SKYDANCING
AEROBATIC FLIGHT TECHNIQUES

SKYDANCING
AEROBATIC FLIGHT TECHNIQUES

DAVID ROBSON

FOREWORD BY THE FRENCH CONNECTION

A Focus Series Book
Aviation Supplies & Acadamics, Inc
Newcastle, Washington

SKYDANCING—Aerobatic Flight Techniques
by David P. Robson

Aviation Supplies & Academics, Inc.
7005 132nd Place SE
Newcastle, Washington 98059-3153

Published 2000 by Aviation Supplies & Academics, Inc.

Printed in the United States of America

03   02   01   00   5   4   3   2   1

ISBN 1-56027-389-5
ASA-SD

Cover Photo—CAP 10B of The French Connection by Tony Ambrose
Graphics and Layout: Aviation Theory Centre Pty Ltd, Melbourne, Australia

Contents

Foreword

We have never met David Robson. However, we feel we know him. Reading about his life and reading his book, we found someone with a lot of experience who was willing to share that experience and his passion as well. After retiring from the Air Force, he could have joined the airlines or the industry and made a bundle of money. He chose teaching instead. He chose to pass on, to new pilots, all he had learned through his very rich life as a pilot.

Sometimes we hear that, although general aviation is actually safer than years ago, probably due to better aircraft, maintenance, navaids and airway systems, the level of flying skills is actually decreasing. What is happening, we believe, is that many instructors are very young and some only do that job for a couple of years in order to accumulate the number of hours to get into the airlines. As a result, some young instructors tend to teach how to pass the test rather than teaching flying skills, because they do not know any better. Although most try to do their job well, even if it is a temporary job, they have neither the experience nor the luxury of a senior instructor to supervise them and help them with their students. By the time they become good at teaching, they are leaving for the airlines. Many of these young instructors are teaching the next generation of instructors and this is one reason why the level is deteriorating. Often, we have mentioned that the solution to better teaching would be to have all veteran airline pilots, or veteran aviators in general, spend some of their time coaching new instructors, flying with them and their students so as to help them to better teach the basic skills. David Robson did this and it is so refreshing.

We enjoyed reading David's book and found in it much valuable information. We hope everyone reading this book will enjoy it just as much as we did. Thank you David for taking the time and making the effort to share your knowledge.

Daniel Heligoin and Montaine Mallet
French Connection Airshow, Mudry Aviation Ltd.

Dedication

Monsieur Auguste Mudry is one of the great men of French aviation. Indeed he has been called the Enzo Ferrari of France because of his lifetime dedication to the manufacture of the best-handling aerobatic aircraft in the world. I was fortunate to be able to meet Mr. Mudry on several occasions when I was selecting aircraft for the Australian Aviation College. He and his staff welcomed me and I had the pleasure to tour his factory and his old chateau in Normandy.

Avions Mudry produced world-class competition aerobatic aircraft, and the very best aerobatic training aircraft, the CAP 10B. The CAP 10B was developed from the Piel Emeraude as a basic trainer for the French Air Force. The design has been so successful that it has remained in production for 25 years without major change. The wings of the CAP 10B are covered with plywood skins, which are spliced with the same care and precision as a violin. The aircraft were built at a rate of one per month and Mr. Mudry was able to visit the factory every day and personally inspect (and pat) each aircraft as it was built. I was privileged to know Monsieur Mudry, to fly his aircraft and to share his Calvados.

Avions Mudry is no longer, but the aircraft continue to be built at a new facility, CAP Aviation in Darois, France.

David Robson (in the CAP 231) with Monsieur Auguste Mudry

Author

David Robson is a career aviator having been nurtured on balsa wood, dope (the legal kind) and tissue paper. He made his first solo flight in a De Havilland Chipmunk shortly after his seventeenth birthday. He made his first parachute jump at the age of sixteen. His first job was as a junior draftsman (they weren't persons in those days) at the Commonwealth Aircraft Corporation in Melbourne, Australia. At the same time, he continued flying lessons with the Royal Victorian Aero Club. He joined the Royal Australian Air Force (RAAF) in 1965 and served for twenty-one years as a fighter pilot and test pilot. He flew over 1,000 hours on Mirages and 500 on Sabres (F-86 with a Rolls-Royce engine). He completed the Empire Test Pilot's course at Boscombe Down in England in 1972, flying everything from gliders, to the magnificent Hunter, Canberra and Lightning. He completed a tour in Vietnam with the United States Air Force, as a Forward Air Controller, flying the O 2A—*Oscar Deuce*.

He was a member of the seven-aircraft formation aerobatic team, the *Deltas*, which flew his favorite aircraft, the Mirage fighter. This team was specially formed to celebrate the fiftieth anniversary of the RAAF.

After retiring from the Air Force, he became a civilian instructor and lecturer. During 1986-88 he was the editor of the *Aviation Safety Digest* which won the Flight Safety Foundation's international award. He spent over ten years at the Australian Aviation College as the Chief Instructor, Director of Pilot Training and Manager, Business Development. The college had 35 airplanes and trained over 1,000 cadet pilots for the world's leading airlines. He introduced the Mudry CAP 10B aerobatic training aircraft to Australia. In 1998, he was awarded the Australian Aviation Safety Foundation's Certificate of Air Safety. He loves airplanes, aerobatics and instructing—and he still dreams of, one day, flying a Spitfire.

Acknowledgements

My thanks to:

David Pilkington, who has been in the aviation industry since 1966 when he started flying and became an aeronautical engineering student at RMIT, then later at Cranfield College of Aeronautics. His flying interests are purely aerobatic—Australian Advanced Aerobatic Champion, Pitts aerobatic formation team, low-level aerobatic testing officer, and aerobatic instructor. His flying and engineering interests were combined for the development of the Laser. In 1995, he joined Aviat in the U.S. as Vice President, Engineering, and as test/demonstration pilot for the new Pitts and the Husky. He moonlights on weekends as a flight instructor, teaching aerobatics in anything from the Cessna Aerobat to the Pitts S-2A—in between wringing-out his Laser.

Montaine Mallet is a 50% partner in the French Connection with her husband, Daniel. This superb aerobatic display team, which flies CAP 10 aircraft out of Florida, regularly appears at U.S. airshows including EAA Oshkosh. Daniel and Montaine manage a school specializing in aerobatic courses and emergency procedures training which I would highly recommend to any pilot. I am grateful to Montaine for her valuable advice in the preparation of this book.

Preface

This book is the result of two emotions:
- enthusiasm for flying, and
- concern for incomplete or inadequate pilot training.

A pilot moves in a three-dimensional world and I believe it is negligent not to train a pilot to be able to place an aircraft in any attitude and to recover safely from any attitude. In order to do this, both the training curriculum and the specifications for training airplanes need to be addressed.

Also, aerobatic flight is sheer fun. The thrill, challenge and enjoyment of aerobatic flight is unmatched by any other sport. It is like race-car driving in three-dimensions.

Training Curriculum

I was fortunate to learn to fly on Chipmunks when the flight training syllabus produced a complete, three-dimensional pilot. My military training then reinforced the essential foundation of maneuvering flight and all aspects of precise aircraft control.

Reading about the many occasions where the pilot *lost* control often led me to wonder about their basic flight training. A pilot should never *lose* control. Large aircraft filled with passengers also had *upsets* where the bank angle, and sometimes the pitch attitude, exceeded 90°. Recovery from these situations can be marginal—to say the least.

I watched videos and even witnessed air display accidents that simply shouldn't have occurred. I noticed, in several training manuals, discrepancies in the description and technique for aerobatic flight that simply could not be left unanswered.

Training Aircraft

The ability to properly train a pilot also depends on the availability of a suitable training aircraft. The lack of such aircraft, and the acceptance by licensing authorities of this lack, has had an effect on the completeness of pilot training for the past three or four decades.

The accident rate on our roads is not being contained by further regulation. So, too, it is with aviation accidents. The only way is by better training—and this requires suitable vehicles. Aircraft such as the Tiger Moth, Piper Cub and the Stearman were effective trainers because they developed good hand/eye coordination, an awareness of and a respect for airspeed, a discipline for flight path control and a sensitivity to surface winds. They were a challenge to fly accurately and well. They instilled correct habit patterns and responses—essential to the automatic correction of flight path or airspeed deviations.

The touring aircraft that currently populate the majority of the world's training fleets are not suitable trainers for other than cross-country and procedural training. For the preparation of this book, indeed for the past ten years, I was fortunate to have access to the CAP 10 airplane, which has all of the attributes of the classic trainer.

Consequently, the descriptions in this book are biased toward the behavior of this aircraft. Obviously, your aircraft will have individual characteristics which will require variations in the techniques or entry speeds. However, the principles remain the same.

Airmanship

Why Talk About Airmanship?

The complete pilot training *package* includes learning how to recognize and control attitude—not only that of the aircraft but also that of the pilot. The pilot's mental attitude is what we used to call *airmanship*. I will always remember a special issue of *Flying* magazine, published in the 1960s, which explained, very well, the importance of both types of attitude. It had a great effect on my flying career.

Aviating is a motor skill and it is a form of motor sport. Airmanship could be called *aeronautical sportsmanship*—it's about following the rules of the game, fair play, striving for higher standards, staying safe, being responsible and courteously sharing the sky with other airplane *drivers*.

I hope that flight instructors will keep alive the concept of airmanship. Otherwise, we are in danger of losing the skill, status, respect, courtesy and pride in our very special profession of aviation.

Introduction

Why Learn Aerobatics?

The practice of aerobatics develops sensitivity, feel, judgment and anticipation.

A railcar or locomotive can move in two directions but in only one dimension, backward or forward, along its track. A motor vehicle or a boat can move in two dimensions, backward, forward, left and right (making their own tracks). A submarine can move in three dimensions albeit in a limited way—no inverted flight (hopefully). Only an aircraft can truly move in three-dimensional space. Yet, most pilots never learn how to fully maneuver the aircraft in this three-dimensional space. Certainly, we can takeoff, climb, turn, descend and land, but that's a very small part of the total flight envelope of which most aircraft, and most pilots, are capable.

Learning aerobatics, not only allows you to explore the full envelope of the aircraft, it considerably enhances confidence in your own ability and that of the aircraft.

Student pilots, having learned the basic aerobatic maneuvers, noticeably improve in their general handling of the aircraft. Aerobatic pilots develop a feel and sensitivity for their airplane and a de-sensitivity to maneuvering flight. They develop an instinctive awareness of attitude and the quickest way back to straight-and-level, controlled flight.

Because an aircraft maneuvers in three-dimensional space, a pilot should be capable of placing the aircraft into any attitude and recovering safely from any attitude.

There have been several instances, even with an aircraft the size of a Jumbo, where autopilot malfunctions, volcanic eruptions or upsets due to wake turbulence have put the aircraft in a situation where the bank angle has exceeded 90° and the pitch attitude has reached 30° or more, nose down. A pilot who has undergone even the basics of aerobatic training is more likely to recover correctly. There have been instances where this training has led to a successful recovery. Also, the probability of recovering safely and without further damage to the aircraft is enhanced.

Most importantly, a good reason to learn aerobatics is the sheer enjoyment of it all. There is nothing more exhilarating than flying an aerobatic aircraft and putting together a smoothly coordinated, balanced, and well performed sequence of aerobatic maneuvers.

Aerobatics develop respect for the aircraft and yourself—your abilities, your capabilities and your limitations. Aerobatics is exciting flight. No pilot should miss the opportunity to at least fly the basic, positive-*g* maneuvers.

Go for it.

Aerobatic Wisdom

There is no situation in aerobatic flight from which you will not be able to recover—provided you respect your limitations, and those of your airplane, and you *never* allow yourself to get into a position of having insufficient altitude.

Don't fly with, or learn from, anyone who is not a qualified aerobatic instructor.

Don't perform aerobatics in an aircraft that is not specifically approved for aerobatics.

Don't commence an aerobatic maneuver unless you are certain of completing it above your approved minimum altitude and with sufficient remaining energy to zoom.

Don't commence maneuvering without a prior self-briefing or mental preparation.

Don't commence maneuvering without briefing your passengers.

Don't commence maneuvering without completing the HASELL checks and clearing turns or wing-overs.

Don't commence maneuvering unless you know the required horizontal and vertical airspace is clear of other aircraft.

Don't perform ad-hoc or ad-lib sequences—nor beat-ups.

Don't maneuver a new airplane without a check pilot or at least at a safe altitude which allows for unexpected responses.

Don't spin an aircraft unless you are familiar with its correct (and perhaps, unique) entry and recovery procedures, and you are certain it is correctly loaded.

Don't perform aerobatics, especially prolonged spinning, with any medical condition (especially a head cold), without adequate sleep, or if you have a hangover.

Chapter 1

Terminology

Aerobatic flight has its own terminology which isn't quite universal. Let's introduce a few of the common terms.

General Terms

Departure (From Controlled Flight)

Any situation where the flight path deviates from the direction commanded by the pilot's control input or where the aircraft responds in a manner contrary to the normal, expected response to a particular control input.

Load Factor

The total load or force on the aircraft caused as a result of both gravity and centrifugal reaction — measured in multiples of the force of gravity, or *g*. In scientific papers, load factor may be represented by the symbol "Gz."

Rolling *g*

The non-symmetrical load factor experienced by each wing, when simultaneously rolling and pitching, caused by the aileron deflection, in addition to the applied *g*.

Wing-Root Bending Moment

The total bending at the wing-root caused by the total lift force being generated by the particular wing. When pitching, both wing-roots experience the same bending moment. When the aircraft is also rolling, the wing-root bending moment is increased on the wing with the downward deflected aileron as the outboard section of this wing is generating more lift, the center-of-pressure is displaced further out from the wing-root and therefore causes a greater bending moment. This is why it is dangerous to simultaneously roll wings-level when pulling out of a spiral dive.

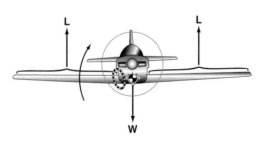

Wing Root Bending Moment

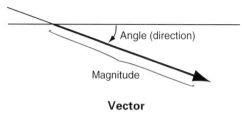

Vector

Vectors

A vector shows the magnitude and direction of a force or path. Thus the flight path vector could be a climb at 100 kt or a 3° approach path at 80 kt. The lift vector is always at right angles to the flight path and the magnitude for our purposes is in multiples of the force gravity (*g*)—which is the same as multiples of weight.

Components

Every force can be resolved into components:
- either a horizontal and vertical component, or
- perhaps a component along the flight path and one at 90° to the flight path.

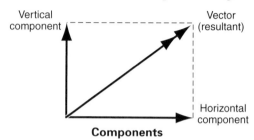

Components

Resultant

Several forces can be combined into one resultant—thus for a turn, gravity and centrifugal reaction can be combined into a total force which must be overcome by the wings—and in a climb the forces of drag and the component of weight against the direction of the flight path have to be balanced by the thrust to sustain the climb path angle and speed (vector).

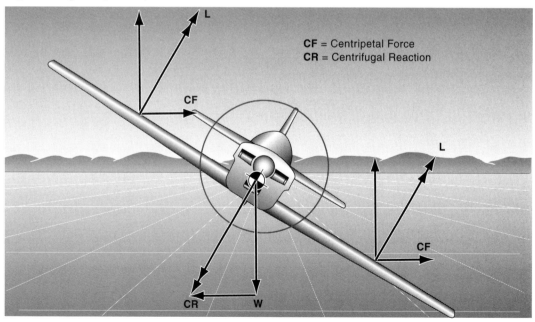

Centripetal Force

Centripetal force is the force that changes the flight path. The change is in the direction of the applied force. To turn, a force must be applied, towards the center of the turn. This force, supplied by excess lift from the wings, is called *centripetal* force.

Centrifugal Reaction

To every *action* there is an equal and opposite *reaction*. Thrust is the reaction to the propeller or jet engine pushing air rearward. Centrifugal reaction is the reaction to centripetal force. It causes the pilot to be pushed into the seat.

Airspeeds

V_A maneuvering speed—the speed above which full control deflection is to be avoided. This speed is generally a factored margin above stall speed to ensure that full control deflection will result in a stall before exceeding the structural limits of the airframe. Because it is a factor above stall speed and stall speed varies with gross weight then the value of V_A increases with increasing weight. For a normal category aircraft with a limit of +3.8 *g* then V_A is approximately double V_S. For an aerobatic aircraft V_A may be 2.5 to 3 times V_S.

V_{NO} maximum airspeed, normal operations—the maximum speed for normal flight operations. This speed should only be exceeded, with care, in smooth air.

V_{NE} maximum speed, never exceed—the maximum speed that is not to be exceeded under any circumstances.

V_S the power-off, stalling speed, clean (flaps and landing gear up).

Simple Aerobatic Maneuvers

Rolls

There is no such thing as a simple roll. The following are the common types:

Aileron Roll

A roll nominally about the longitudinal axis of the aircraft, usually a fairly rapid roll and with a straight flight path. It is normal to raise the nose before beginning the roll so there is upward momentum to carry the aircraft through the roll without loss of altitude.

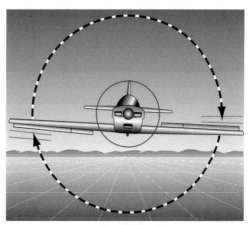

Aileron Roll

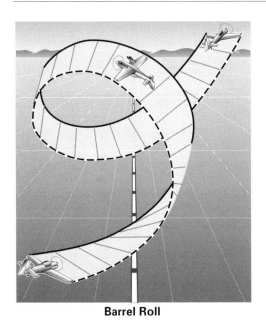

Barrel Roll

Barrel Roll

A combination of rolling, pitching and yawing whereby the aircraft follows a helical flight path as if it was flying around the inside of a barrel.

Slow Roll

A roll around the longitudinal axis while the aircraft follows a nominally straight-and-level flight path. The roll is deliberately conducted at less than maximum roll rate so that there is a need for deliberate sideslip (knife-edge flight) to maintain altitude with the wings vertical and a need for deliberate negative angle-of-attack to maintain the inverted level path. Note that a slow roll does not imply low airspeed.

Hesitation Roll

A roll with distinct pauses—usually at the 90° points (four-point hesitation roll) although some use eight or even more points. The roll-rate is quite rapid to accentuate the pauses. It takes sudden and large control inputs to achieve the distinct and accurate hesitations.

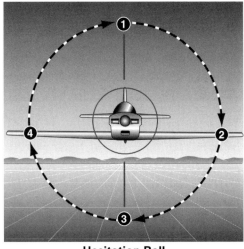

Hesitation Roll

Snap Roll (Flick Roll)

An accelerated stall and incipient spin through a half or one turn, sometimes more—usually along a horizontal flight path although it is not uncommon in a vertical, or 45°, upward or downward direction. Also used for the half roll or complete roll at the top of a loop to make an avalanche or an Immelmann.

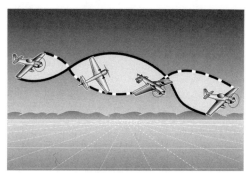

Snap Roll

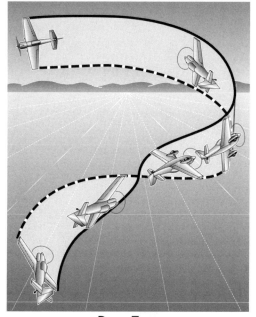

Derry Turn

Turns

Derry Turn

A roll-under reversal of a steep turn from one direction to a steep turn in the other direction—normally made via an aileron roll but sometimes via a snap roll.

Inverted Turn

An inverted, or outside turn, from straight-and-level inverted flight with the pilot's head outside the flight path (so there is negative *g* throughout).

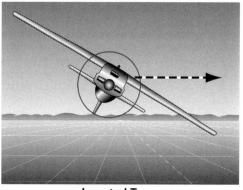

Inverted Turn

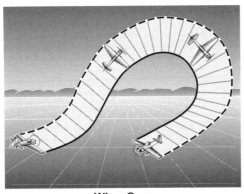
Wing-Over

Wing-Over

A gentle pull up, roll, climbing turn, descending turn, change of direction, through any number of degrees—used to position the aircraft and to establish the entry parameters for the next maneuver. Very useful for lookout and for gaining the feel of a new aircraft. Not strictly an aerobatic maneuver as all aircraft are capable of a wing-over. Can be joined to form a lazy eight.

Chandelle

The chandelle is similar to the first part of the wing-over but is completed at the highest point and lowest speed—the apex of the maneuver. It is a means of exchanging airspeed for altitude while changing direction in a small radius. It was derived from the Immelmann which is based on the first half of a loop rather than the first half of a wing-over (*see* Immelmann, Page 9).

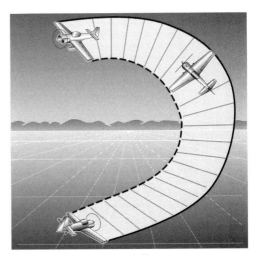
Chandelle

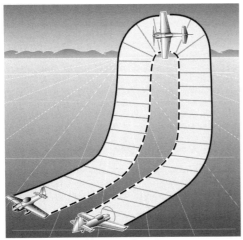
Hammerhead

Hammerhead

The hammerhead consists of a straight pull up, to the vertical, a yaw through 180° from vertically upward flight to vertically downward flight and then a straight pull out to recover in the opposite direction.

Loops

A loop is a maneuver entirely in the pitching plane in which the aircraft rotates through 360° in a nominally circular path.

Normal Loop

The normal loop has positive *g* applied throughout and has a nominally constant pitch rate.

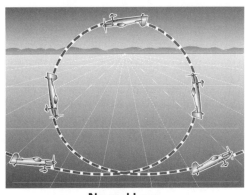

Normal Loop

Square Loop

In a square loop the pitching is conducted in four discreet flight path changes of 90° with a momentary period of straight flight in between corners. It is a severe maneuver requiring rapid *g* application and removal to make the maneuver distinct and clearly defined.

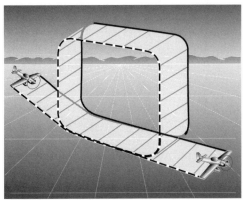

Square Loop

Avalanche

The avalanche consists of a complete snap roll from inverted flight to inverted flight at the top of the normal loop. It is spectacular yet easy and comfortable to perform.

Outside Loop

The loop performed with the pilot's head "outside" the flight path (that is, negative *g* throughout). It requires an inverted entry and ends inverted. It takes some experience and recency to perform.

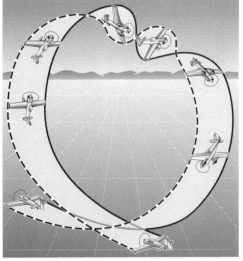

Avalanche

Complex Aerobatic Maneuvers

Eights

Horizontal Eight

A three-quarter loop to a vertical dive followed by a half roll (through 180°), a loop from vertically down to vertically down followed by a further half roll and pull out.

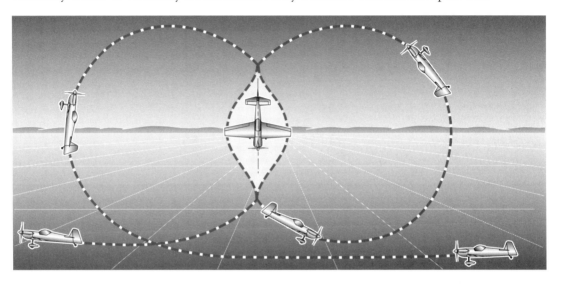

Cuban Eight

A ⅝ loop (through 225° to the 45° downward position) followed by a half roll, a further part loop through 270° (45° down to 45° down), a further half roll and pull out.

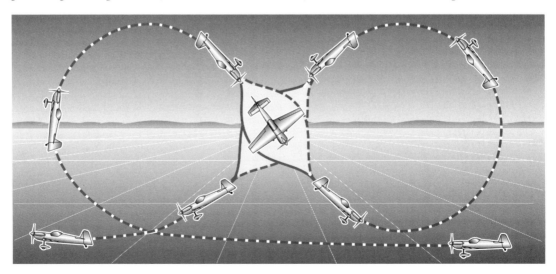

Vertical Eight

A normal half-loop to inverted with a half roll, another loop upwards, a further half roll to inverted and completion of the first loop.

Clover Leaf (Whifferdill)

Four loops with 90° downward (or upward) rolls in between.

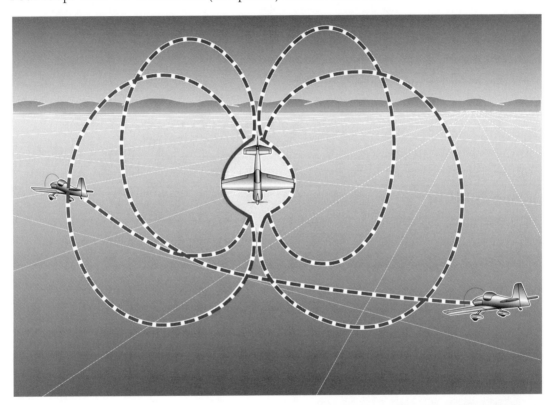

Immelmann

A half loop with a half aileron roll or half snap roll to erect flight at the top. A change in direction in the vertical plane with no horizontal component (developed by WW1 fighter pilot, Max Immelmann).

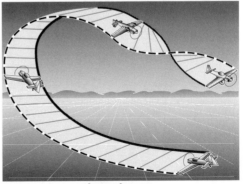

Immelmann

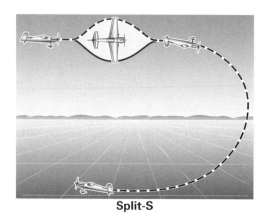
Split-S

Split-S (Half Roll and Pull-Through)

A half aileron roll or half snap roll to inverted flight followed by the downward half of a loop to erect flight.

Vertical S

A half roll, then a downward half loop followed by a further half roll and half loop. The vertical S can also be performed upward, as a half loop to inverted flight, half roll, further half loop to inverted and a further half roll to erect flight—a half of a vertical eight.

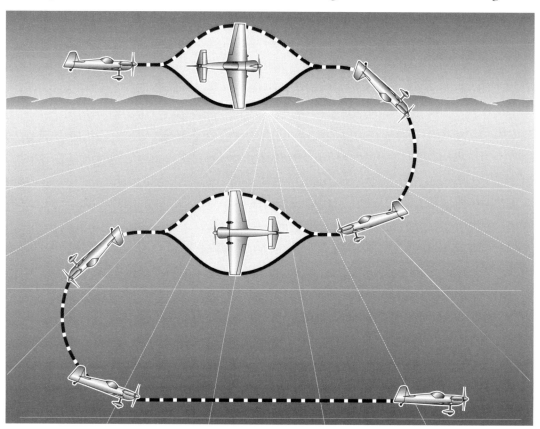

Knife-Edge Flight

A straight-and-level flight path with the wings vertical. The side-force from the fuselage together with the vertical component of thrust generates the necessary lift.

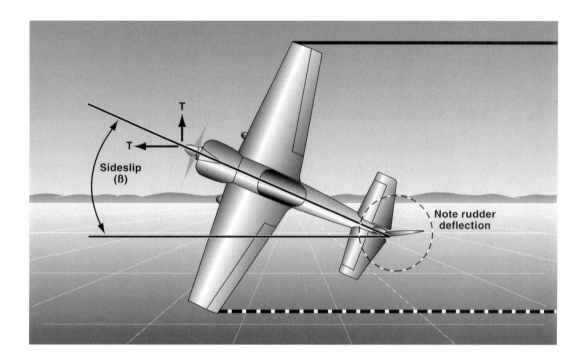

Sideslip (also β, *beta*)

The lateral angle between the longitudinal axis of the fuselage and the relative airflow—in any attitude.

Angle-of-Attack (also α, *alpha*)

The angle between the chord line of the wing and the free-stream relative airflow.

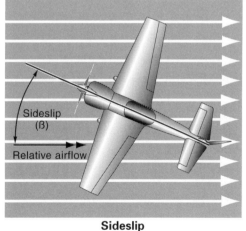

Sideslip

Spins

Spin or Stable Spin

A balance of aerodynamic and gyroscopic (inertia) forces and moments which cause a sustained, low airspeed rotation in yaw, pitch and roll (possibly with some oscillatory motion), and the aircraft following a spiral or helical flight path with a nominally vertical axis. For an aircraft designed for spinning, this is also a stable spin.

Unstable Spin

A spin where the forces are not balanced—resulting in an oscillation in roll, pitch and/or yaw. Airspeed may fluctuate and eventually increase to a point where one or both wings are unstalled and the aircraft accelerates into a spiral dive.

Flat Spin

A spin whereby the controls are applied to increase the rate of rotation. As a result, the inertia (gyroscopic) forces are enhanced (built up) to cause a higher angle-of-attack and pitch attitude in the spin (therefore the term, flat spin). The increased rate of rotation usually causes a prolonged recovery time. Some aircraft will not recover from a flat spin. Hence the importance of strictly maintaining the recommended control positions in the spin—as determined for your aircraft type.

Pro-Spin

Any control deflection that maintains the spin, that is, left aileron in a right spin is both *out-spin* (opposite to the direction of the spin) and *pro-spin* as it helps to sustain the spin. (Some aircraft vary.)

Anti-Spin

Against the spin, that is, left aileron in a left spin is *in-spin* (in the direction of the spin) yet *anti-spin* as it tends to initiate spin recovery.

Inadvertent Inverted Spin

Inverted spins are beyond the scope of most aerobatic trainers and beyond the scope of this book. The inverted spin is simply a departure from controlled inverted flight—either from straight-and-level or turning, during an outside loop or vertical maneuver. Be especially careful of rolling to inverted at too slow a speed during an Immelmann when you arrive with *nothing on the clock*. It can also happen as a result of inappropriate control inputs in an erect spin.

Chapter 2

The Aerodynamics Behind Aerobatics

An aircraft moves in three-dimensions—forward, backward, up, down, left and right. Motion in a straight line is called *linear* motion and it may be at constant speed or changing speed. As well as changing speed in a straight line, an aircraft can also change direction—in a temporary or sustained way, and in a sudden or gentle way. The process of changing direction is known as *angular* motion. The motion or rotation takes place around the balance point of the aircraft—known as the center of gravity.

To describe the angular motion, we separate the components into three individual planes or axes. The axes and motions are described as:
- rolling (in the rolling plane)—rotation about the longitudinal axis;
- pitching (in the pitching plane)—rotation about the lateral axis; and
- yawing (in the yawing plane)—rotation about the vertical, or *normal*, axis.

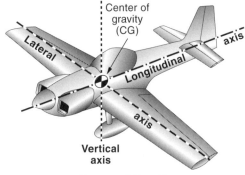

Center of Gravity

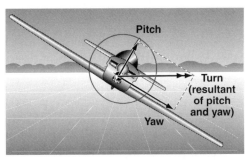

A Turn Comprises Pitch and Yaw

Some maneuvers are performed by motion solely in one plane (for example, a loop is pitching through 360°, an aileron roll is rolling through 360°) or one plane at a time (for example, hammerhead, 90° pitching, followed by yaw through 180°, followed by pitch through 90°). More often a combination of two or three motions is involved (a turn is a combination of pitching and yawing while a barrel roll is rolling and pitching with some yaw, and a spin is yawing, pitching and rolling with perhaps some oscillation).

A balanced turn is a combination of pitching and yawing with zero sideslip. However, some maneuvers may involve deliberate sideslip (for example, slow roll, knife-edge flight, Immelmann and spin)—some of which involve very high sideslip angles.

The Perfect World—No Gravity

Maneuvering in a zero-*g* world only requires the wings to generate the external reaction to change the flight path. At zero-*g*, zero lift is required to remain airborne. A loop would simply require a set stick position to maintain an angle-of-attack and the aircraft would fly around the loop at constant speed, constant pitch rate and constant *g*.

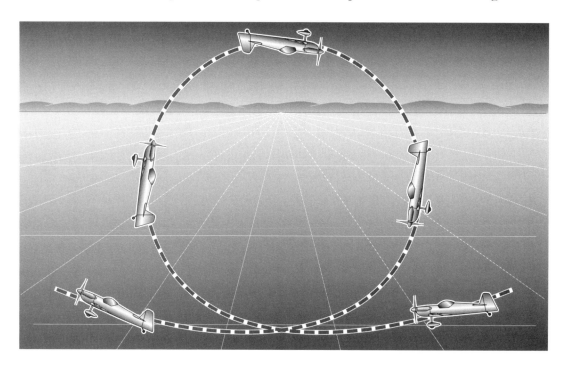

A roll would occur around the longitudinal axis of the aircraft at zero angle-of-attack. No sideslip would be required at the 90° positions and no forward pressure (no negative angle-of-attack) would be required when inverted.

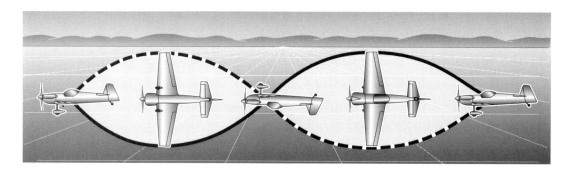

A turn could be completed with 90° of bank with all lift being used to turn and no component needed to stay aloft. In fact, a turn with less than 90° of bank would result in a climb.

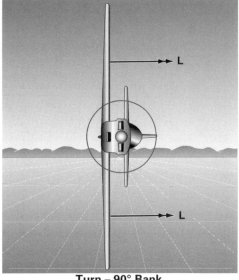

Turn – 90° Bank

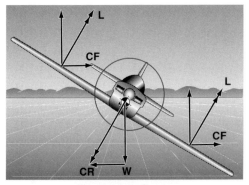

Forces in a Turn

When you add the force of gravity there is a continuing need to generate a force to remain airborne as well as the force to maneuver. If you add gravity and don't correct the rolling maneuvers, the flight path curves downward.

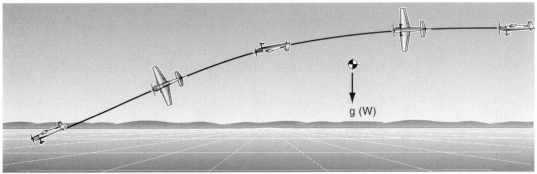

At every stage in any maneuver an upward force is required, or the flight path and/or the speed will change.

For the loop to be round there has to be a changing amount of total *g* so that a constant value of *applied g* is maintained. Let's apply +3*g*.

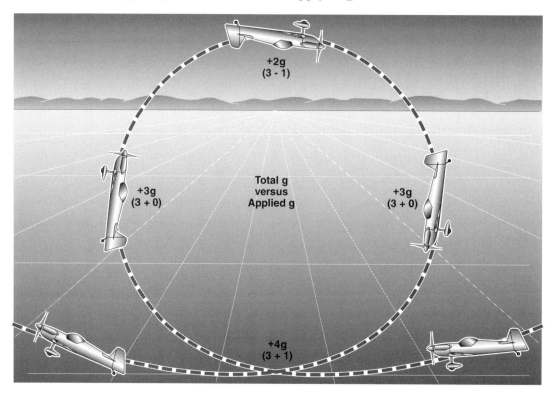

+2g
(3 - 1)

+3g
(3 + 0)

Total g
versus
Applied g

+3g
(3 + 0)

+4g
(3 + 1)

But even then, the speed is going to vary unless the thrust is also varied. And since the amount of thrust is generally limited, there is an inevitable speed variation. Thus the shape of the loop cannot be round unless there is a further adjustment to carry the aircraft over the top.

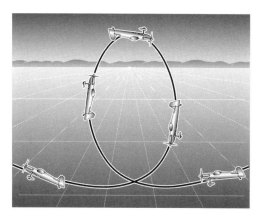

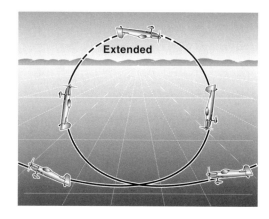

Extended

In the case of the roll, there is a need to sustain an upward force equal to the force of gravity throughout the maneuver. Thus there is a positive angle-of-attack on entry, sideslip at the 90° positions, and a negative angle-of-attack at the inverted position.

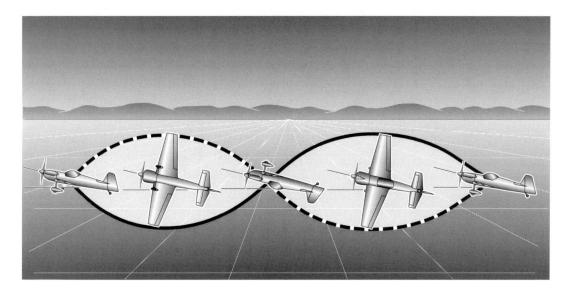

The aircraft still rolls around its longitudinal axis but elevator and rudder pressures are required to generate the sideslip and negative angle-of-attack while the ailerons roll the aircraft.

Many aircraft cannot sustain the level flight path during this extreme maneuver and so it is common to raise the nose and establish an upward flight path at the beginning of the maneuver. The upward momentum allows a slightly curving path which does not leave the aircraft in an unacceptably nose-low attitude and a descending path at the end of the maneuver.

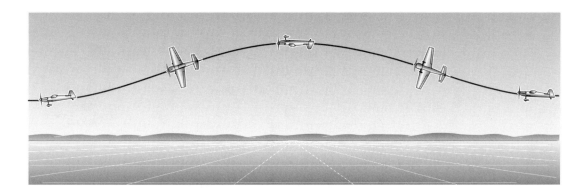

What is a Turn?

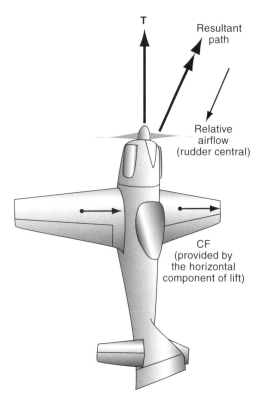

Turning is a combination maneuver of pitching and yawing and no rolling except on entry and exit. Therefore aileron is not required to maintain the turn (except to balance power effects) unless there is sideslip to cause a rolling moment. There is no sideslip if the balance ball is centered with the rudder.

What Causes the Turn?

Pitching is caused by the elevators (back pressure) and this causes the increased angle-of-attack to generate the excess lift to change the flight path. The horizontal component of lift provides the centripetal force to change the flight path.

The balance can be caused by the rudder or by sideslip:

- The turn can be done by banking and applying back pressure and allowing the sideslip to cause the yaw. In this case the ball will be displaced.

SLIPPING TURN

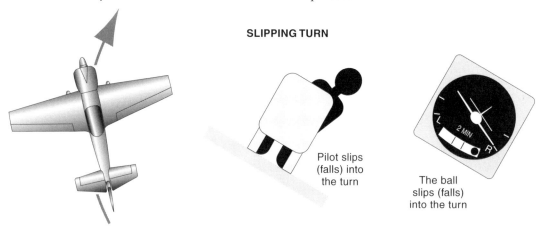

Pilot slips (falls) into the turn

The ball slips (falls) into the turn

- Alternatively, the rudder can be used to balance. In this case, there is no sideslip and the balance ball is centered.

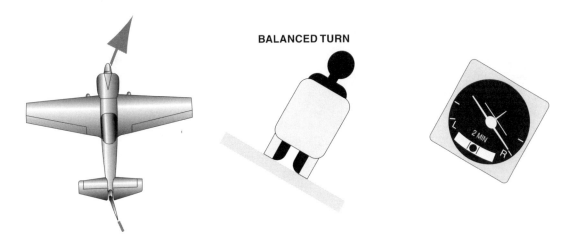

BALANCED TURN

Hence, even a jet needs some rudder to balance a turn even though there is no engine torque to be countered. However, a jet has a very large vertical stabilizer and high directional stability, so even a very small amount of sideslip causes the balance in the turn. Thus the ball is very nearly centered even when rudder is not applied. Additional rudder may also be needed during the entry and exit to balance any yawing moment caused by aileron deflection, especially at low airspeeds (high angles-of-attack).

Which Control Does What?

As the bank angle is increased, the ratio of pitching to yawing changes. At 45° of bank there is equal amounts of pitching and yawing.

At 90° of bank there is all pitching and no yawing. A typical steep turn or a maximum rate turn in a light airplane is performed at 45°–60° of bank and thus it is mostly pitching, requiring a large amount of back pressure—and very little rudder to generate the small amount of yawing required.

At these very high bank angles, most of the available elevator deflection is required to maintain the high angle-of-attack (close to the critical angle) and pitch rate. If the nose attitude drops, then the amount of extra back pressure to raise the nose is considerable. It is therefore far easier to reduce the bank angle while maintaining the back pressure to bring the nose back up.

Additionally, if the aircraft has insufficient thrust, the only way to maintain best maneuvering speed is to use gravity to assist and therefore sacrifice altitude for airspeed (potential energy for kinetic energy). In this case, again with the wing close to the critical angle-of-attack, the pilot holds the back pressure constant and "plays" the bank angle to raise and lower the nose attitude to maintain airspeed.

Attitude, Angle-of-Attack and Flight Path

It is important before analyzing the aerobatic maneuvers that we distinguish some terms and understand some significant elements. It is vital to distinguish between the terms *attitude, flight path* and *angle-of-attack*.

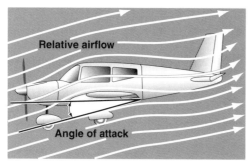

Descending Flight Path; Level Attitude

The *attitude* of the aircraft is the position of the nose in relation to the horizon. This aircraft has a:
* level attitude; with a
* descending flight path.

The *flight path* of the aircraft is the direction it is traveling relative to the horizon. This aircraft has a:
* level flight path; but
* a nose–high attitude.

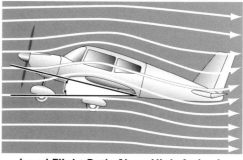

Level Flight Path; Nose-High Attitude

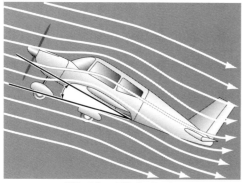

**Climbing Flight Path;
Very Nose-High Attitude**

The *angle-of-attack* is the angle of the wing to the relative airflow. This aircraft has the same angle-of-attack, but also a:
* climbing flight path; and
* a very nose-high attitude.

Note: Each of the aircraft shown has the *same angle-of-attack* with an increasing pitch attitude and with descending, level and climbing flight paths respectively.

The *attitude* of the aircraft is where it is *pointing* (not necessarily where it is *going*).

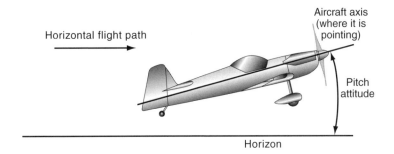

The *flight path* is where it is *going* – and it can be referenced to the airflow, to the horizon (as is usual), or to a point on the ground, a runway or display line (for approach and landing or for display aerobatics respectively). This latter path also takes into account the effects of wind. The difference between these references is very subtle but very significant.

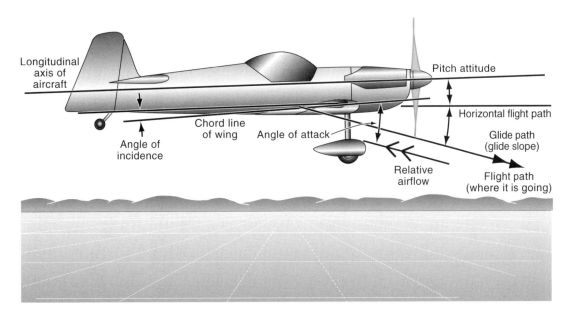

Airspeed is speed through the air. *Groundspeed* is speed relative to the earth and therefore includes the effects of wind. Speed relative to the earth is the measure of absolute speed. Groundspeed determines the *momentum* and the *kinetic energy* of the aircraft.

The only way to adjust the flight path to reach a point on the ground, against the wind, is to increase the thrust. *Thrust* is the means to overcome drag (plus gravity in some situations) and headwind. Thrust *sustains* the flight path.

How Does an Aircraft Maneuver?

Any change of speed or direction is caused by generating a force in the direction the pilot wishes the aircraft to go.

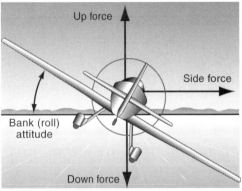

Forces in a Turn

Newton correctly observed that:

- a body will continue in its state of rest or uniform motion in a straight line, unless acted on by an external force; and
- the rate of change of momentum is proportional to the applied force and takes place in the direction in which the force acts, that is, the direction and speed will change in the direction it is pushed and the rate of change is proportional to the amount of push.

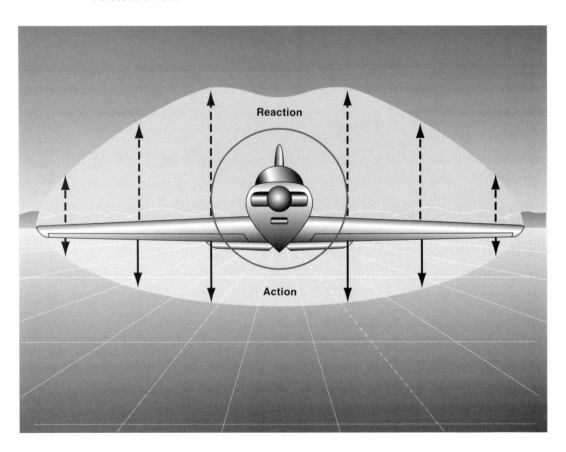

The pilot can cause the aircraft to accelerate or decelerate by changing thrust or by using gravity (by diving or climbing)—but the only way to change the direction of the flight path is to generate an external force in the required direction. In the absence of vectored thrust, the pilot can only use excess lift from the wings to push the air and cause a reaction in the way he wishes to go. So the potential to generate excess lift is the potential to maneuver.

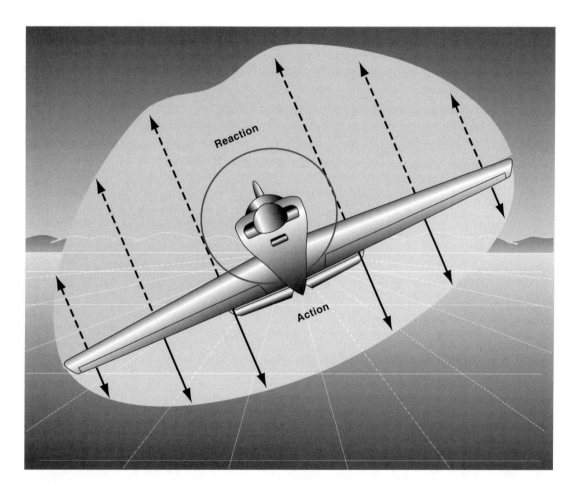

Note: *excess* lift—if there is no excess lift over that required to stay airborne, then there is no force available to change direction. When flying at V_S you cannot maintain level flight and also turn. There is some misunderstanding that the minimum-radius turn occurs at the slowest speed. In practice, it does not and it cannot. Best turn occurs at the critical angle-of-attack and the minimum radius occurs when the critical angle is reached at the limiting load factor. At V_S you have no maneuver potential—none, *zero*.

The ability to maneuver depends on airspeed above the stall (more correctly, the angle-of-attack margin below the critical angle). At any speed, the pilot can apply elevator deflection to the point when the critical angle is reached and beyond which the wing will stall. At very low speed, the wing is already close to the critical angle and so the potential for excess lift is low. At higher speed, the angle-of-attack is low and the margin to the critical angle is great—so there is plenty of potential excess lift available to maneuver. The limit then becomes one of available thrust or the structural limits of the airframe.

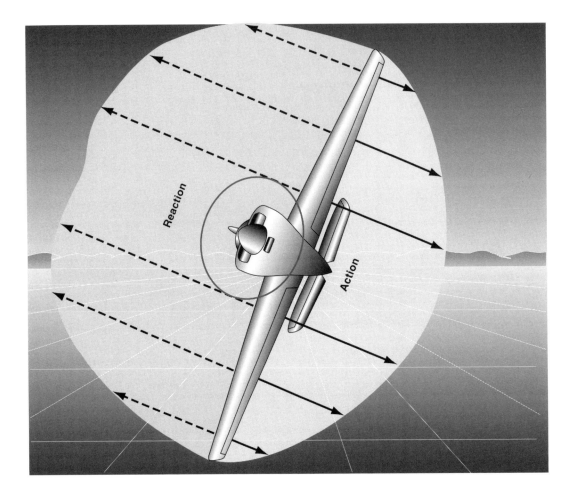

At V_A the critical angle is nominally reached at the point when the positive load factor limit is also achieved, for example, at twice the stall speed the pilot can apply $+4g$ and no more. For an aircraft to be able to reach a maximum limit of say, $+9g$, the airspeed has to be at or above $3 \times V_S$. Below this speed, the wing will reach the critical angle-of-attack; that is, it will stall before being able to reach the structural g-limit.

Zooms, Climbs and Dives

You will be familiar with terms like *climb*, *dive*, *zoom* and *roll*, but now we need to be more specific about their precise meanings so you can understand what is happening to the aircraft. Any aircraft can follow almost any flight path for a moment or two. If we accelerate a Jumbo to its maximum speed we could gently pull up to a very steep angle. We would be gaining altitude but we would not be climbing because we would not be able to sustain the climbing path. The airspeed would be falling—rapidly. This temporary exchange of airspeed for altitude is called a *zoom-climb* or *zoom*.

In the opposite case, a *descent* or *glide* can be sustained and the speed controlled. A *dive* is a descending flight path where the speed is increasing.

Thus when we are maneuvering, we are using a combination of both temporary and sustainable maneuvers to position the aircraft, but it is the sustained maneuvers (a function of the aircraft's excess thrust) that ultimately allow us to perform a sequence of aerobatics within a specified altitude band.

The Nature of Maneuvering

Natural Laws

Maximum Performance Maneuvering (Flight at the Limits)

It is one thing to pull suddenly on the control column to reach $+6g$, but it's an entirely different matter to be able to sustain a load factor of $+6g$. *What limits it?*

The ability of an aircraft to maneuver is ultimately limited by:

- excess (spare) lift;
- excess (spare) thrust; and
- structural strength.

The relevant limit depends on the actual flight condition at the time, for example, above or below V_A, light or heavy weight and flap and landing gear configuration.

Additionally, the human pilot may impose limits on the maneuver capability of the aircraft because of physiological limits or lack of training and recent practice. This is an important and wise precaution—too often ignored.

To maneuver, that is, to change the flight path in a particular direction, requires a force to be generated in that direction. The pilot has four forces at his disposal and thus four forces by which the flight path can be changed. They are thrust, weight, drag and lift. The most powerful force available to the pilot is the lift force and the pilot has the means to direct this force by banking and to control the amount of lift by changing the angle-of-attack.

To change direction, the pilot needs to create a force toward the center of the maneuver. *Centripetal force* is equivalent to the piece of string that you need to rotate a stone around your head. Without the string, the stone departs in a straight line.

An aircraft is the same:

- To accelerate forward, you can increase thrust or you can dive and use the force of gravity.
- To climb, you can increase thrust or change flight path by increasing lift momentarily and then use momentum to carry the aircraft a limited vertical distance.
- To decelerate, you can either reduce thrust, increase drag (with speed brakes or landing gear extension) or raise the nose and use gravity to slow yourself down.
- To change the direction of the flight path sideways, you can bank and use part of the lift force (a component of the lift force) to generate the centripetal force to cause the turn while maintaining a vertical component to balance the force of gravity.
- To loop, you use the excess lift to generate centripetal force to change the flight path continuously around the maneuver.

A simple roll (aileron roll or slow roll) does not need a centripetal force as the flight path does not need to be changed. All that is needed is a rolling moment (a twisting force caused by the ailerons) while the aircraft proceeds along its original flight path. However this is not the case for the barrel roll. The barrel roll does have a changing flight path around a spiral, so both rolling and pitching moments, as well as centripetal force, are needed. There is a need for a rolling moment from the ailerons and a pitching moment from the elevators—and there is a need for a sustained centripetal force toward the central axis of the barrel.

For a loop, the aircraft uses momentum from the dive to sustain the initial climbing path and maximum thrust to offset the induced drag and the force of gravity—to allay the airspeed reduction. Over the top, gravity will help the flight path change and only a small centripetal force is needed. On the downside, drag is needed to contain the acceleration and thrust reduction; speed brakes and induced drag (pulling harder) can be used for this purpose.

An aircraft with sufficient excess thrust (more thrust than weight and induced drag combined) can pull up and sustain the looping maneuver from any speed—but this is exceptional.

Energy

Aircraft with limited thrust can compensate by use of other means to allow a limited maneuver potential that is beyond its normal capability. Stored energy in the form of spare altitude over your minimum *(potential energy)* or spare airspeed over V_S *(kinetic energy)* provides you with the capacity to maneuver. It's like having a credit rating or money in the bank.

Zoom potential is money in the bank to be used when needed. Spare altitude gives potential energy which can be converted into speed and spare speed can be converted into altitude. Thus, don't ever be low and slow—especially in an aircraft without much excess thrust. You have nowhere to go; no reserves to play with. If you are low and have excess speed you have excess lift (to turn) or momentum (zoom potential) to climb.

See how people become trapped in valleys. They are low already and then they slow down to allow more reaction time or in the belief that they can maneuver better (more tightly) at a lower speed. But then they have neither the capacity to maneuver nor to zoom—no ability to turn or to zoom over a hill, even into clouds at an angle higher than the rising terrain. At low speed, the induced drag is already high, they are closer to the stalling angle with little excess lift available and they are in an aircraft without much excess thrust. It's nowhere to be and there's nowhere to go.

A motor vehicle can turn at very slow speed because it is sitting on the ground, and it doesn't need to generate lift. It is limited at higher speeds because there is a loss of tire friction to generate the high centripetal force required (that is, it will skid). This is not the same as the aircraft. The very best turn that an aircraft can perform is at a speed where the wing reaches its critical angle-of-attack at the maximum allowable load factor. For a training aircraft (non aerobatic), this is approximately twice the stall speed. There is no value in being slower than this. Whether this turn can be sustained in level flight is a matter of excess thrust, but in this situation a 180° turn is the most you need and perhaps you can sacrifice a little spare altitude (if you kept any).

Newton's law of motion, and how the wing generates excess lift to cause the flight path of the fuselage and its occupants to be changed, has been discussed. Let's now examine the control of that lifting force and its effects on the structure of the aircraft. The aircraft's ability to change the flight path and speed depends on the ability of excess lift and excess thrust. Conversely, the aircraft's performance limits are determined by its maneuver potential, again excess lift and excess thrust until, of course, you reach either the structural limits of the aircraft, the airspeed limits or your own limit. Let's look at these in turn.

Excess (Spare) Lift

In straight-and-level flight, lift equals weight. If you are flying close to the stall speed, the wing is close to its stalling angle and therefore there is not much spare capacity to generate additional lift. The margin to the stall is small, therefore the aircraft's ability to maneuver at speeds close to the stalling is extremely limited.

If you are in straight-and-level flight, at twice the aircraft's stall speed, the wings are capable of generating four times the amount of lift that they can generate at the stall speed. If it needs one magnitude of lift to balance the weight, then there are three spare amounts of lift with which you can maneuver the aircraft. Its maneuver potential is a total of 4g. If you were flying at three times the aircraft's stall speed, the amount of lift that can be generated is nine times the weight, or 9g. Therefore, your maneuver potential, at any particular time, is determined by your excess airspeed, that is the margin above the stall speed. This excess lift determines your capability to instantaneously change the flight path of the aircraft. To sustain a changing flight path, you also have to take into account induced drag and therefore your ability to counter that drag; thus the next factor that determines your maneuver potential is the amount of available excess thrust.

Excess (Spare) Thrust

The high angle-of-attack necessary to generate 6g brings with it induced drag. The ability to sustain a maneuver depends on the excess thrust available and also the direction of the maneuver in relation to the force of gravity. Yes, gravity is still there.

In a level turn at 6g, gravity is part of the total force that the wings have to overcome—the wings are countering gravity and generating a centripetal force to change the flight path. At the bottom of a loop, gravity also adds to the required force needed to change the flight path whereas at the top of a loop, gravity helps. This is why the First World War fighters used the Immelmann; they fought gravity at the beginning when they had excess speed and used gravity to help them at the top when they had little excess.

We know that the aircraft's angle-of-climb is proportional to its excess thrust. Having overcome drag, the amount of spare thrust determines how steeply you can climb. When you are maneuvering an aircraft, you are increasing the angle-of-attack of the wing. When you increase the angle-of-attack of the wing, you generate induced drag—a drag that is induced as a result of making lift.

The amount of induced drag is dependent on angle-of-attack, but also for a given design, it depends on aspect ratio (actually the spanwise distribution of lift or weight in relation to span) and to a lower extent, the shape or planform of the wing. Thus a highly-loaded stubby wing with square tips has very high induced drag. A biplane may have even more.

Elliptical Wing

You have probably read about the Spitfire with its elliptical wing planform.

An elliptical wing is more complex and more expensive to manufacture than a wing with a constant section, because all of the ribs are different and you have compound curves. However, the benefit in flight is significant. The almost perfect spanwise distribution of lift combined with the small wingtips reduces induced drag. This means that the aircraft can maneuver without substantial loss of performance.

Conversely, an aircraft with straight, constant section wings has a very high induced drag. It may be fast but it slows when it turns. A small aerobatic training aircraft generally has to climb to altitude before maneuvering and loses altitude throughout an aerobatic sequence, even with the use of full power.

The significance of this induced drag is illustrated by the Avions Mudry CAP 10 with its elliptical wing. Although relatively low-powered, it can complete an aerobatic sequence without loss of altitude and, if managed properly, can even climb throughout.

Structural Limits

As you have seen, to maneuver the aircraft, the pilot increases the angle-of-attack of the wing and the wings apply a force to change the direction of the fuselage. This force is transmitted through the point of attachment of the wings and is felt as a force which also tries to bend the wing. This is called the wing-root bending moment.

Incidentally, a flying wing has no wing-root bending moment because the load is spread over the wing rather than concentrated in the fuselage and thus can have a much lighter structure and withstand the same high loads.

The ability of the structure to withstand the g forces is primarily dependent on two factors:
- the ability of the wing-root and any additional struts or bracing wires to absorb the wing-root bending moment, and
- the structural strength of the horizontal stabilizer for vertical loads and the vertical stabilizer for side-loads.

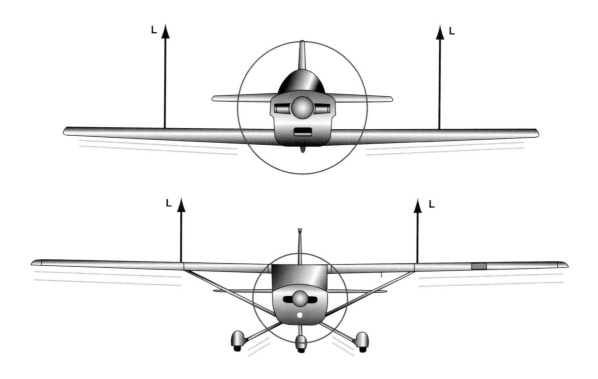

An aerobatic training aircraft is designed to allow the pilot to apply $+6g$ and $-3g$. (An aircraft in the utility category approved for limited maneuvering may be designed to $+4.5g$ and $-1.5g$.)

Both the horizontal stabilizer and the wing-root are designed to allow these loads to be reached as an everyday occurrence without permanent deformation nor structural damage. The vertical stabilizer and rudder also have to be able to withstand the high side loads associated with knife-edge flight and flick maneuvers (if approved).

Another consideration is the ability of the control surfaces and trim tabs to withstand tail-slides—something for which many aircraft are not designed and therefore such maneuvers are prohibited.

To provide a safety margin, the structure is in fact designed and tested to at least 1.5 times this value. While the structure may suffer some damage or permanent deformation, the structure must not suffer failure unless 1.5 times $+6$ or 1.5 times -3 (that is, $+9g$ or $-4.5g$) is exceeded, even for a short time. The reason for this margin is to allow the pilot to fly to the published limits and to keep a reserve of structural strength in the event that he flies through turbulence, or applies additional control deflections which cause the loading to be non-symmetrical. However, above the normal limit, some damage may occur and it may be expensive to repair.

Think about the loads that the engine mounts are having to carry also!

Rolling *g*

Imagine an aircraft pulling out of a straight dive and the pilot applying $+6g$. Each wing is trying to bend upward from its root. Because it's a straight dive, each wing is generating the same amount of lift and each wing-root is experiencing the same bending moment.

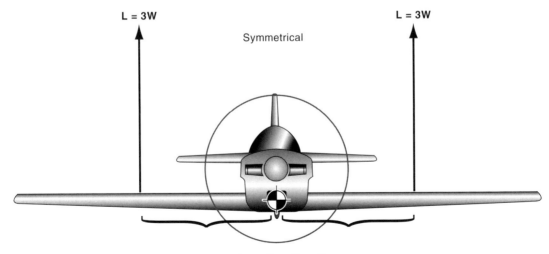

Wing Root Bending Force

If at the same time as applying the $+6g$, the pilot now applies full aileron deflection, the change in camber and therefore the amount of lift generated by each wing is changed.

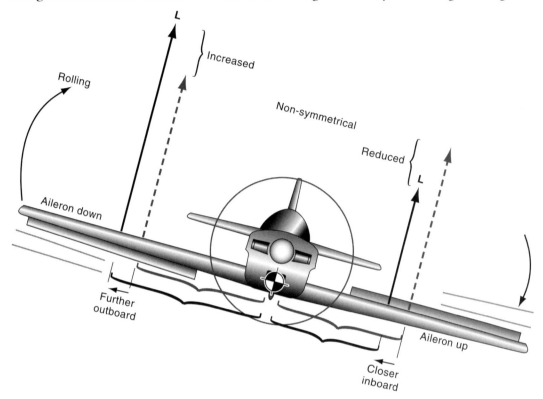

The wing that has the aileron deflected downward is generating more lift than the symmetrical case, and not only that, the center of the lifting force is further outboard on the wing because the outboard section is doing more of the work. It has a higher angle-of-attack or greater camber. Therefore, that wing and wing-root are experiencing a bending moment beyond the $+6g$ of the symmetrical pull out. The other wing, with the aileron deflected upward, has a reduced amount of lift and the center of lift is moved inboard because the outer part of the wing is doing less work. Therefore, its wing-root bending moment is considerably reduced.

This imbalance in load factor due to aileron deflection is called *rolling g* and there is no indication of it in the cockpit. So, to ensure that you don't exceed the normal $+6g$ limit, you must reduce the load factor whenever you want to simultaneously apply aileron deflection. As a guide, you should not apply full aileron deflection if the aircraft is experiencing a load factor in excess of two thirds of the limit for symmetrical flight. That is, if the aircraft is designed to a pilot limit of $+6g$ symmetrical, you should only apply full aileron deflection during maneuvers at load factors below $+4g$. This allowance also applies to negative, rolling-*g*, maneuvers.

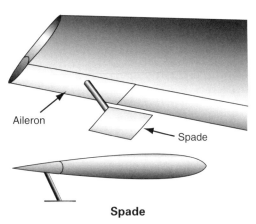

Aileron

Spade

Spade

Spades

The development of fighters in World War II allowed higher and higher airspeeds to the extent that control forces became excessive. The size of the aileron surface needed to provide high rates-of-roll was causing very high control loads. Spades were developed to allow the large surface but to reduce the control force. They act as an aerodynamic balance. They were successful, but soon after, powered control systems were developed and the spades disappeared. They have been reintroduced in several competition aerobatic aircraft.

Gusts

An aircraft which flies through a changing current of air will momentarily feel the added gust as an increase or reduction in applied g depending on the orientation of the gust. If the aircraft is pulling up for an Immelmann at $+6g$ and flies through a thermal with a strong vertically-upward current, then the aircraft will be overstressed.

The aircraft will have another speed known as turbulence penetration speed or V_B which is the recommended speed for flight in turbulence. An aircraft maneuvered in such an atmosphere should be flown at a safe margin below the g limits. An aircraft at the critical angle-of-attack and at high g that flies through a vertical gust could experience an accelerated stall and departure from controlled flight.

Any applied load is additive—that is to say any load due to gravity, maneuvering or turbulence, adds up to the point where either the aircraft could stall (below V_A) or could be overstressed (above V_A). This applies to both symmetrical flight and to rolling g. Neither an accelerated stall nor overstress is acceptable in aerobatic flight and so the only protection is for the pilot to leave a margin of g or angle-of-attack below the limits. When maneuvering in turbulent air or when there is a possibility of vertical gusts or windshear, then the pilot should stay within two-thirds of allowable limits.

Pilot Limits

There are absolute limits beyond which damage will occur and there are pilot limits.
There are two *pilot* limits:
- factored structural limits to which the pilot can routinely fly, while maintaining a safety margin below absolute structural limits; and
- the pilot's personal physiological limits, discussed in the next chapter.

Flight Envelope

We mentioned that the ability of an aircraft to maneuver is limited by:
- the amount of excess lift it can generate;
- the amount of excess thrust; and
- the structural limits (aircraft or pilot!).

Provided we have excess speed above the stall, we have excess lift available to us but at any speed, that lift is limited by the fact that the wing will ultimately reach its stalling angle or critical angle-of-attack. At any time during maneuvering flight, the pilot has enough control power to increase the angle-of-attack of the wing to its stalling angle (provided it is loaded within normal limits). It will then either reach the structural limit of the aircraft (at speeds above V_A) or at lower speeds, it will reach the stalling angle, beyond which it rapidly loses its lifting capability. For each aircraft, there is a published flight envelope and for some this is generally portrayed in what is called a V-n diagram.

The V-n Diagram

The V-n diagram shows the flight envelope of the aircraft in terms of its minimum speeds, its maximum speeds, its maximum load factors (positive and negative) and where in the envelope the limit occurs. If you look at the diagram, you will see the upper structural limit defines the line across the top of the envelope, the limiting speed defines the right hand boundary, the limiting structural strength for negative g determines the lower boundary, and the converging lines on the left-hand edge are dictated by the wing reaching its positive, or negative, stalling angle-of-attack.

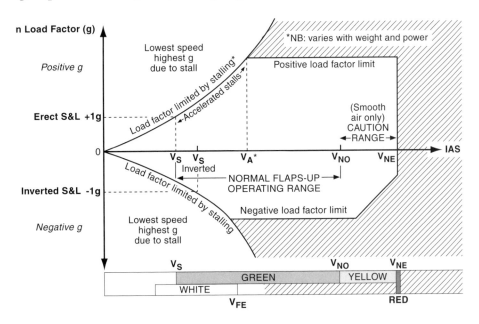

Thus, for each speed, there is a corresponding limit, which below the corner point, is determined by stall, and above it by structural restrictions. This corner point represents a speed known as maneuvering or V_A. It is the speed below which the pilot can apply full control deflection without exceeding the structural limit of the aircraft. That is to say, it is the point where the aircraft will stall before it will reach the limiting load factor. It is vital to know the V_A speed for your aircraft. Note that it is based on the clean, power-off stall speed and therefore varies with configuration, power and gross weight. Your aircraft may have a range of values for V_A for different weights.

Load Factor Limits

In the training aircraft you've flown previously, you would have felt small amounts of *g* during steep turns, perhaps as much as +2*g* if you did a 60° bank, level, turn. For aerobatic maneuvering, you will regularly experience +4*g*, perhaps a little more. Aerobatic aircraft should be installed with an additional instrument to show exactly what load factor the aircraft is experiencing.

Accelerometer

The *g* meter, or accelerometer, simply has a small bob-weight on a spring. The more the aircraft maneuvers, the more the spring is stretched, and the more the needle is deflected. It shows both positive and negative *g* and has two *tell-tale* needles which are deflected to show, at the end of the flight, the maximum, positive and negative *g*, reached during that flight. These needles are resettable for each flight. If ever you get into an aircraft and any of the needles show an amount of *g* in excess of the normal limits, then don't take that aircraft until it is checked for structural damage.

It is wise for aerobatic training aircraft to have two *g* meters, one of which cannot be reset except by the maintenance engineers. That way any overstress is recorded and inspected before the meter is reset and the aircraft flies again. There are now electronic flight recorders available that record the loads and the number of applications. These are a wonderful development for managing the safe use of aerobatic aircraft.

Obviously, an aerobatic training aircraft needs to be able to sustain flight loads that can be expected in normal aerobatic maneuvers—plus they must have a reserve for safety. For an aerobatic aircraft, the structure is required to withstand a pilot limit (what the pilot is *allowed* to apply—as distinct from what the pilot can *tolerate*) of +6*g* and −3*g*—there must be no permanent damage or deformation of the structure unless +6*g* or −3*g* is exceeded. A 1.5 safety margin ensures that no catastrophic failure occurs unless +9*g* or −4.5*g* are exceeded. This is called the ultimate load factor limit. Rolling *g* limits are two-thirds of these. A competition aerobatic aircraft could have ultimate limits of perhaps + and −12*g*.

An aircraft in the utility category (14 CFR Part 23) will have a limit of $+4.5g$ and $-1.5g$ with the same 1.5 margin. Some aircraft may be both normal or utility category depending on the number of persons, fuel and baggage. It is vital to observe the particular limits (weight and CG) for the utility category, before the aircraft is maneuvered or spun. Be particularly careful to observe weight and CG limits for smaller aircraft such as the Cessna 150/152 or Tomahawk.

Maneuvering Efficiently Within the Limits

Let us consider the V-n diagram and the boundaries that it offers. When the wing approaches the stalling angle, we can generate no further lift and therefore the aircraft is said to be lift-limited or we've reached the lift boundary. To sustain maneuvering flight, for example a level steep turn, we have to increase thrust to match the induced drag, otherwise the airspeed will decay during the turn. If the aircraft has sufficient excess thrust to maintain airspeed, at that particular value of g, then the aircraft could continue there all day—no loss of speed, no loss of altitude. However, only the high performance aircraft, such as the competition aerobatic airplanes, or combat aircraft have this amount of excess thrust.

For most aircraft, the ability to sustain a maneuver is limited by excess thrust and this forms the thrust boundary. For example, an aircraft that has a low aspect ratio generates a massive wingtip vortex and therefore, very high values of induced drag. Delta-winged aircraft, such as the Mirage, even on full after-burner, could not maintain a level turn on the buffet, without losing performance. Despite the high thrust available, the airspeed would decay because of the enormous induced drag at high angles-of-attack.

The only way aircraft can maintain a turn under these circumstances is to lower the nose and use gravity to maintain airspeed—thereby sacrificing altitude (potential energy) for airspeed (kinetic energy).

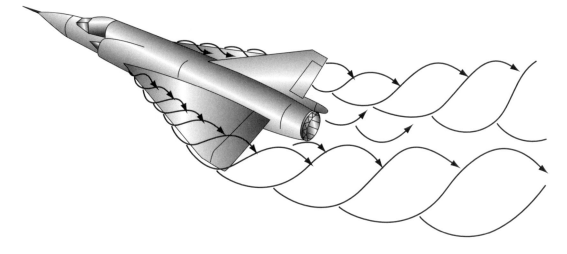

Conversely, the pilot is able to exchange airspeed for altitude. So if the aircraft is flying along at three times its stall speed, it can apply $+9g$ instantaneously or it can zoom, perhaps to several thousand feet. This is what energy management is all about. The finesse of aerobatic flying is to manage the energy during the sequence so that the aircraft completes the sequence with the expected level of energy, that is, the best speed and altitude, perhaps even the same level of energy as it began. Most aircraft are not capable of doing this and one generally has to begin maneuvering with an excess of energy to be able to complete the sequence at a safe speed and altitude.

Pilots of single-engined, propeller–driven aircraft, especially with short wingspan and high power (the aircraft, not the pilot), also have to take into account the gyroscopic forces and torque reaction due to the engine and propeller rotation. Maneuvers will be considerably easier in one direction than the other and piloting technique may have to be modified for maneuvers in the opposite direction.

The Roller-Coaster and Centripetal Force

Now to the barrel roll. It is a special case because it is deceptively easy and because it is still largely misunderstood. Many texts on aerobatics show the highest point of the barrel roll being when the wings are vertical, and that the aircraft passes the wings-level, inverted position when the aircraft is passing the entry level on the downside. Some even say that the aircraft should be pointing at the reference point when the aircraft passes the wings vertical position.

None of this is correct. Gravity won't allow it and not even Mr. Newton could fly it. The ultimate result must be to fall out of the bottom of the maneuver. It is a danger-ous mis-conception and has been the proba-ble cause of several air-display accidents. (Display pilots and formation leaders, believ-ing this technique, have *pulled* the nose down after the wings-vertical position. This virtu-ally ensured that there was insufficient alti-tude to complete the roll, and in the case of low-altitude display flying, meant that they inevitably impacted the ground.)

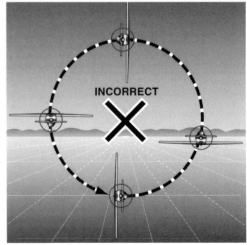

Incorrect Representation of Barrel Roll

If the pilot tries to follow the simplistic view of the roll, there is great danger that it will be impossible to prevent the rapidly descending path through the second half of the roll. Unless the aircraft is capable of a much higher roll-rate, the pilot may not be able to recover before ground impact.

INCORRECT

Gravity

Incorrect Representation of the Barrel Roll

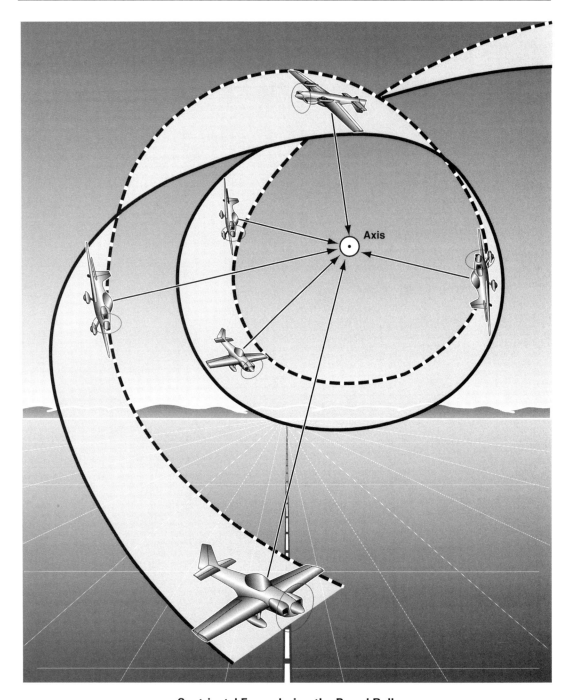

Centripetal Force during the Barrel Roll

Inverted Dive

There is a further insidious effect of the nose-down inverted position during the second half of the barrel roll, or indeed during the inverted, speed-increasing part of any maneuver. Natural stability of the aircraft causes the nose to pitch-up with increasing airspeed. In erect flight this has the effect of containing the airspeed and restoring the status quo. If the aircraft is inverted and accelerating then the stability is now pitching the nose up with respect to the pilot's view but nose down with respect to the earth. Thus the dive steepens and the aircraft will not assist recovery. Only the pilot can change the trend by rolling upright or applying negative *g*.

You may have read about the *victory roll* performed by fighter pilots as they returned from a successful mission with a *kill*. They would join the traffic pattern and then perform the roll. So many died from this maneuver that it was eventually banned—as was the *garbage roll* after takeoff with the landing gear and flaps down. It was a terrible waste of life—because the pilots did not understand the nature of the rolling maneuver and the danger of the nose being low at the half-way point. Remember that the war-time pilots were relatively inexperienced.

From basic science, we know that there must be a force toward the center of the roll. This is centripetal force and it can only be generated by the wings as excess lift. (Sideforce from the fuselage and vertical stabilizer is relatively small and the sideslip angles would have to be high.) Thus the only practicable way the aircraft can follow the spiral path of the barrel roll is by the wing force being directed toward the central axis of the roll.

There is no other way. Designers of roller-coasters know this so that they don't have the passengers falling-out during the roll.

It is true that the pitch attitude is steepest at the wings-vertical position, but the aircraft still has an upward flight path due to momentum and it reaches the highest point in the maneuver at the wings-level inverted position.

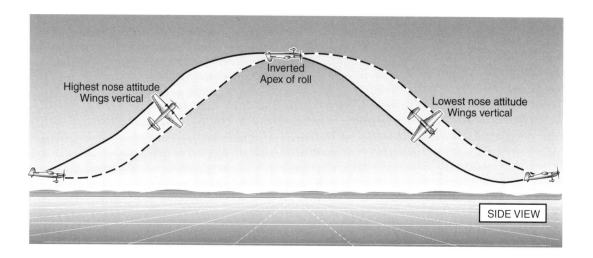

The importance of this relationship between attitude, flight path and the highest point of the maneuver is significant.

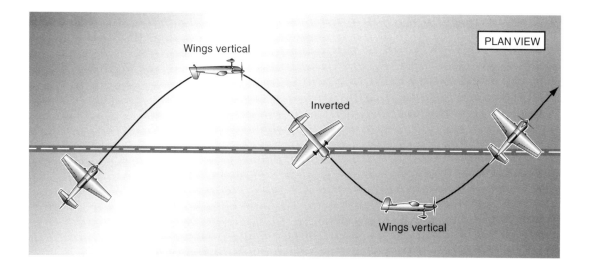

In fact, it is the same as all maneuvers, including the loop.

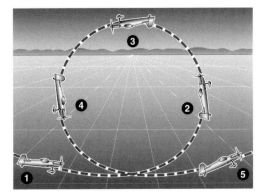

Stages of the Loop

The highest point is half way and the steepest nose-up and nose-down attitudes are at the ¼ and ¾ positions.

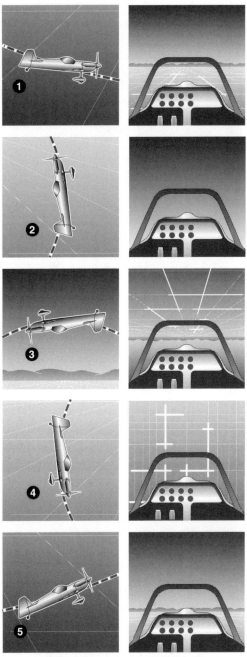

Pilot Views during the Loop

Let's reexamine the attitude at different points of the barrel roll and see where the aircraft is located in the flight path. See how the highest nose attitude is not the highest altitude.

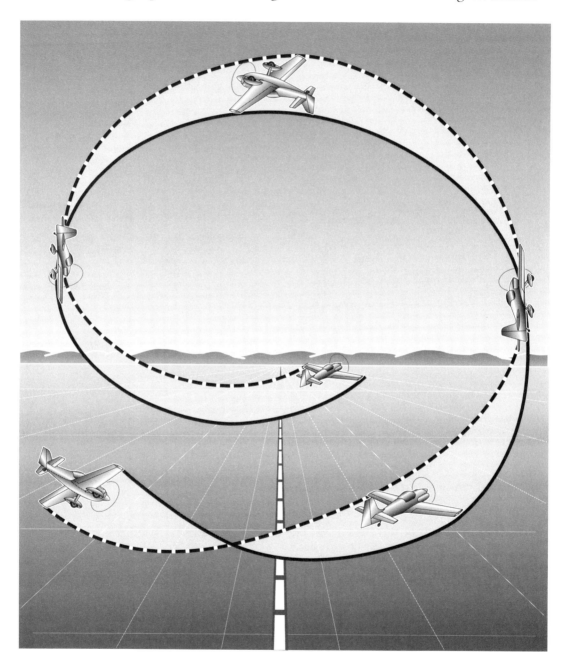

Low Speed Flight

For maneuvering flight, we have to change our personal attitude and ingrained association between airspeed and angle-of-attack. In straight-and-level flight, there is a close relationship. However, in maneuvering flight there is none. We can be at high speed and stall. We can be well below the stall speed and nowhere near the stalling angle. Angle-of-attack is determined by stick position—at any speed. Airspeed affects only the power of the controls and the influence of the stabilizing surfaces.

Stalling

We will begin in straight-and-level flight at low speed. The angle-of-attack is high, the ailerons are sloppy and the power will be fairly high to overcome the induced drag.

We have seen the control column has the power to stall the wing at any speed (except perhaps at the forward CG limit), and at speeds below V_A, there is no risk of exceeding the structural limits. To be able to anticipate the stall, you need now to reconsider your previous training. No longer will an impending stall be indicated by:

- a nose-high attitude (you could be inverted, nose down with full power and still stall the wing);
- sloppy controls (could stall at any speed);
- quiet (any power setting); and
- airspeed (it can stall at any speed).

What do you have left?

The reliable cues are:

- stall warning horn or light (OK, because it is based on angle-of-attack);
- buffet (also based on angle-of-attack);
- stick force (provided you haven't retrimmed); and
- stick position (if the CG is correct).

If the elevators are largely deflected, the angle-of-attack is high—no matter what attitude, speed or power setting.

So we stall by pulling back on the control column and we unstall by releasing that back pressure. It's as simple as that. Negative stalls are caused by pushing on the control column and are avoided by releasing the forward pressure. Once again, leaving the trim set for high-speed cruise improves the feel and the warning we have of how close we are to the stalling angle. If we trim out the force there is less pull force, and so less warning.

Loss and Restoration of Controlled Flight

The terms, *stall, incipient spin, incipient stall, accelerated stall, autorotation, region of reversed command, poststall gyrations,* and *spin* are well encompassed by the U.S. definition, *departure from controlled flight.* This expression was coined to describe any situation where the aircraft did not do what the pilot wanted or did what the pilot didn't want—that is, it behaved in a manner not in accordance with normal expectations to the control inputs that were applied.

Generally, one wing, or a significant part of one wing, has exceeded the stalling angle and depending on the particular aircraft, we can expect uncommanded rolling, yawing and pitching deviations from controlled flight.

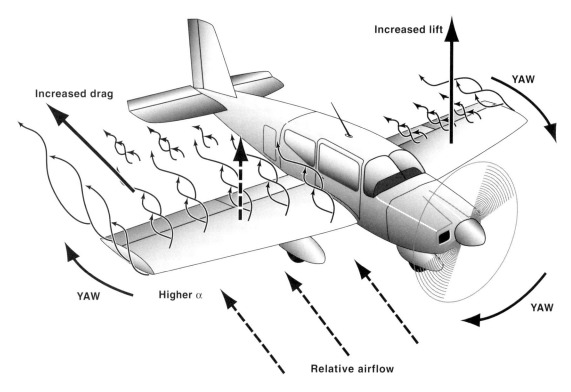

Departure from Controlled Flight

Several aspects are consistent throughout all departures from controlled flight. We have to be at or close to the stalling angle. There has to be a control input, sideslip, roll-rate, yawing moment, torque, slipstream or gust that causes one wing to go *over the edge*. Any subsequent attempt by the pilot to restore the flight path by conventional control inputs can aggravate the situation and actually cause the reverse of what is required, for example, using aileron to pick up a stalled wing will cause it to deviate further and faster. Thus the response is *uncommanded*. The aircraft autorotates.

As well as the change in angle-of-attack due to the deflected ailerons, the presence of adverse aileron yaw can cause a yawing moment which itself will accentuate any departure tendency.

The simple solution in all cases is to take both wings clear of the stall by reducing the angle-of-attack. Then all controls will once again respond conventionally.

Stop the yaw and stop the sideslip. There will be no spin. Reduce the angle-of-attack. There will be no stall.

Any dynamics that have developed will disappear after a few oscillations, when the angle-of-attack is reduced. If it all happened in a vertically-upward flight path, then holding the reduced angle-of-attack and allowing the aircraft to accelerate into a nose-down path will see order restored.

Departure From Controlled Flight

Avoiding Loss of Control

If back pressure is partially released as soon as the aerodynamic buffet or the stall warning is evident then there will be no loss of normal control response. In any attitude and at any speed, the wing cannot and will not stall without being forced to. Even exceeding the stalling angle will not result in a departure unless there is an imbalance, sideslip or applied power and even then, the rudder will be effective in preventing any uncommanded roll or yaw.

Regaining Control

In almost every case, control is immediately restored as soon as the angle-of-attack is reduced below the stalling angle for both wings. Any build-up of gyroscopic forces can then be countered in a conventional way.

Autorotation

Recall your theory lessons about autorotation and spinning. As the aircraft departs from controlled flight, the pro-spin forces and moments cause the aircraft to gyrate in yaw, roll and pitch. The rate-of-rotation builds until gyroscopic forces and moments come into play. For a deliberate spin, the pilot's control inputs (full rudder and full back stick) over-ride the aircraft's natural stability and tendency to recover unaided. The aerodynamic forces are subdued and the rotation accelerates. Centralizing the controls is generally sufficient to prevent a spin from developing.

In early aircraft designs, the aircraft could stall asymmetrically simply due to aileron deflection at the stall. Newer designs won't depart unless gross control inputs are applied, and even then, most also require deliberate rudder deflection.

Some aircraft have a tendency, or a greater tendency, to depart if they are stalled with power applied and perhaps with flaps extended.

Spinning

The spin is ultimately a vertically-downward flight path at low airspeed during which the aircraft yaws, rolls and pitches fairly rapidly in a helical path around a vertical axis. In the developed (stabilized) spin, everything builds to a situation where the aerodynamic forces and moments trying to counter the spin are balanced by the gyroscopic forces and moments trying to continue the spin—and all equals all. Gravity ensures the flight path is ultimately downward.

For aerobatic maneuvering, a prolonged spin is not very useful as it consumes energy—the altitude loss does not result in zoom potential as the airspeed remains low. So, other than using it to change direction or lose altitude in a spectacular way, there is no point staying beyond one or one-and-a-half turns. Further, the physiological consequences of spinning beyond 4 or 5 turns can be adverse. There is an deceptive effect on the pilot's vestibular apparatus (balance mechanism) after 4–5 rotations whereby recovery from a spin in one direction can be perceived as the entry to a spin in the opposite direction.

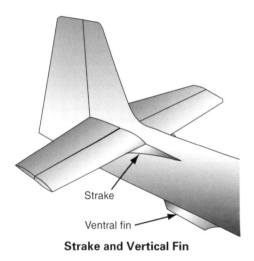

Strake

Ventral fin

Strake and Vertical Fin

Historically, there are stories of almost every aircraft type having had accidents due to prolonged spinning—even after they have been in service for many years. The Tiger Moth had strakes added. The Chipmunk had to undergo extensive trials to discover why it was sometimes very difficult to recover from prolonged spins. It too, adopted strakes. The Robin 2160 received a ventral vertical stabilizer. The Bulldog and Firefly have had some unexplained situations. The Cessna Aerobat and Piper Tomahawk have had spinning accidents which also have not been fully explained.

All of these types are spun very frequently and it may be unfair to highlight what are only occasional problems. However, it seems that prolonged spins allow the gyroscopic forces to build to the extent that recovery becomes more and more difficult or, at least, delayed. Individual airplanes have slight differences in rigging and CG. In some cases, additional recovery measures, such as full forward stick or throttle application to increase rudder and elevator power are necessary. Small aerodynamic effects, such as a slight amount of aileron deflection, can make the difference between normal recovery or not.

Why bother to conduct prolonged spins when the maneuver is of little value anyway, and you have to spend most of the sortie climbing to regain the altitude you have lost?

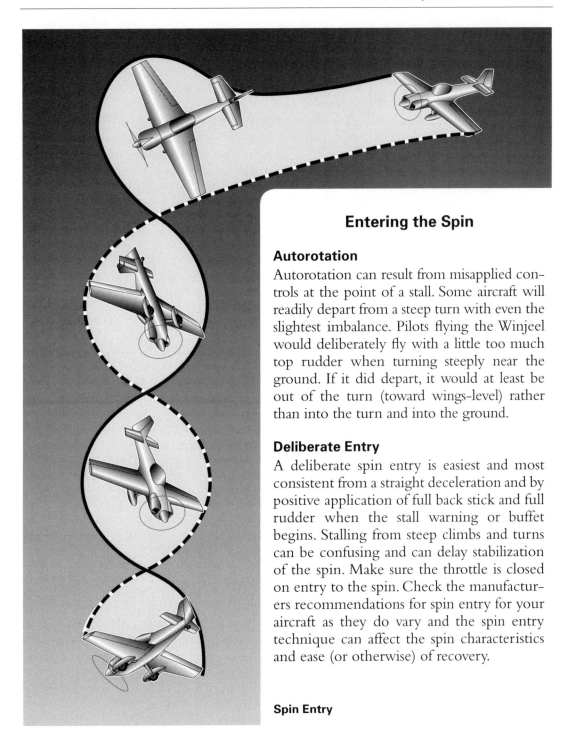

Entering the Spin

Autorotation

Autorotation can result from misapplied controls at the point of a stall. Some aircraft will readily depart from a steep turn with even the slightest imbalance. Pilots flying the Winjeel would deliberately fly with a little too much top rudder when turning steeply near the ground. If it did depart, it would at least be out of the turn (toward wings-level) rather than into the turn and into the ground.

Deliberate Entry

A deliberate spin entry is easiest and most consistent from a straight deceleration and by positive application of full back stick and full rudder when the stall warning or buffet begins. Stalling from steep climbs and turns can be confusing and can delay stabilization of the spin. Make sure the throttle is closed on entry to the spin. Check the manufacturers recommendations for spin entry for your aircraft as they do vary and the spin entry technique can affect the spin characteristics and ease (or otherwise) of recovery.

Spin Entry

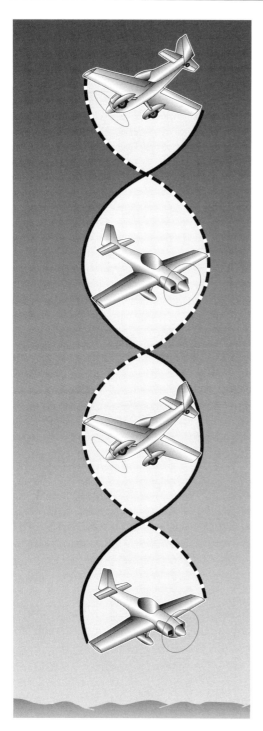

Unintentional Departures

If the aircraft departs from controlled flight, it will not spin if the controls are immediately centralized (especially release back pressure) and the throttle is closed.

This is when we are most likely to be caught-out—from an Immelmann, or when pulling around the corner. The aircraft's natural stability will recover it—if you let it. Even letting go of the controls will probably avoid a spin.

Spin Recovery

There is much discussion about a universal spin recovery technique.

Use the one recommended for your aircraft by the manufacturer.

They do vary because the horizontal stabilizer/rudder geometry and the rudder versus elevator power varies. Some aircraft will recover instantly the controls are released. Some require almost full forward stick. It is important to follow the sequence for your aircraft as to whether rudder or elevator is moved first.

Consider inadvertent entry from a stall with power applied or flaps extended. They will probably delay recovery so it is best to retard the throttle and retract the flaps (and landing gear) as soon as you can.

When you become familiar with your aircraft you will be able to time the recovery inputs so that the aircraft stabilizes in a particular direction and you can use the spin as part of the aerobatic sequence—but generally a two-turn spin is sufficient for this purpose.

Stable Spin

48

The standard recovery from any un-commanded situation or departure (that is, other than a deliberately-held spin) is:

- immediately centralize the controls; and
- close the throttle.

If the aircraft continues to rotate, apply full opposite rudder to the direction of yaw, followed by forward pressure on the control column—until full forward, if necessary. Hold these positions until the rotation stops.

For a deliberately-entered spin, strictly follow the spin recovery technique advised by the aircraft manufacturer. It is important that if they say, *"full forward stick"* or *"briskly move the control column forward,"* or *"apply full opposite rudder, pause, then move the control column forward,"* then that is exactly what you do.

What to do if the recovery doesn't seem to be working? If there is no change in the spin after two turns, confirm the direction of yaw, check the throttle is closed and reapply full rudder opposite the yaw. Then release the stick altogether and consider applying power.

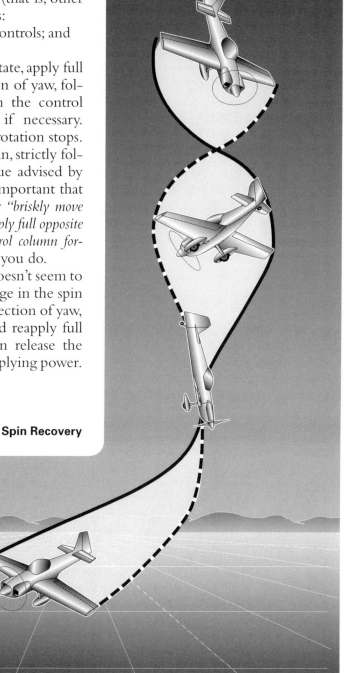

Spin Recovery

Use of Power

Generally the throttle should be closed until the wings are unstalled and the aircraft is accelerating. The gyroscopic moments from the engine and propeller can delay spin recovery or may assist. The slipstream can also be a help—but only use these options if the normal spin recovery is not satisfactory.

Non-Standard Recovery

If the aircraft does not respond, aileron toward the direction of spin will assist recovery. There is also a school of thought which suggests that letting go of the stick is the best recovery technique (with full opposite rudder applied), as a counter to possibly incorrect control inputs (certain aircraft types only). The International Aerobatic Club (which is on the Internet at *http://acro.harvard.edu/IAC/iac_homepg.html*) has much information on, and engages in debate about, spinning.

Control Position (especially if the aircraft has a yoke)

Spinning is a balance of forces and moments. In some aircraft even a very slight amount of out-spin aileron (opposite to the direction of yaw—yet it is pro-spin) will flatten the attitude in the spin, accelerate the rate-of-rotation, and delay recovery. It is vital to have the ailerons neutral during the spin unless your aircraft type requires out-spin aileron to maintain a stable spin (as did the *Winjeel*). Some aircraft also will not remain in a spin unless the stick is held hard back and a relaxation will allow the aircraft to accelerate into a spiral dive.

Direction of Spin

When recovering from a sustained spin it is vital to confirm the direction of spin (the direction of yaw) which in some aircraft can be confused with the direction of roll.

Turn and Balance Indicator

The turn needle of the traditional turn-and-balance indicator (the *bat* of the *bat-and-ball*) will always indicate the direction of yaw in any spin, stable or unstable, erect or inverted. When an aircraft is being tested, an extra panel of instruments is added above the glareshield in the pilot's immediate field-of-view. This always includes a turn-and-balance indicator and an additional altimeter.

The turn coordinator (a similar instrument but with an aircraft symbol instead of a turn needle) has a tilted gyro which indicates both yaw and roll and so can give unreliable readings in a spin where yaw and roll can be opposite (similarly in a limited-panel, unusual attitude recovery).

Also, the balance ball does not indicate the direction of spin and can be displaced in the opposite direction during the incipient stage. The indications can even differ between the left and right side of the cockpit.

Turn Coordinator

Where to Look During a Spin

It is not possible to track a single point on the horizon and watch it come around. Nor is it wise to watch the wingtip. Look ahead to watch the rotation but try to include the upper horizon in your view without trying to follow one point. If you can arrange a very prominent feature such as a runway or lake that can been watched momentarily each time it comes around then it will help keep track of the direction and number of turns.

While spinning has to be learned, it is better to frequently practice recovery from the incipient stage and to use the spin as if it was simply another snap roll. Incipient recovery should become second nature.

Spiral Dive

Firstly, let's state that the spiral dive is a non-event—if you have a clear horizon. The three common circumstances where the situation can be serious, are as follows:

1. The aircraft is trimmed for low airspeed, say in a climb at high power, and the aircraft enters clouds. The untrained pilot allows the heading to deviate and the wings to be slightly banked—only a few degrees. The aircraft enters an almost undetectable turn. As it turns, the outer wing causes the bank to slowly and subtly increase. The nose lowers slightly and the airspeed increases a little. The longitudinal stability (because it is trimmed for a lower airspeed) causes the turn to tighten a little. The rates of roll are below the threshold of the pilot's balance mechanism in the inner ear and so no significant rolling motion is detected.

The turn causes the wing to lift a little more. The trim tightens the turn a little and the nose lowers a little more. The airspeed increases further and the *g* starts to increase. The airflow noise is also building and the airspeed is now increasing noticeably especially in a fast single with a retractable landing gear. Now the pilot starts to feel alarmed, by the noise and building *g*.

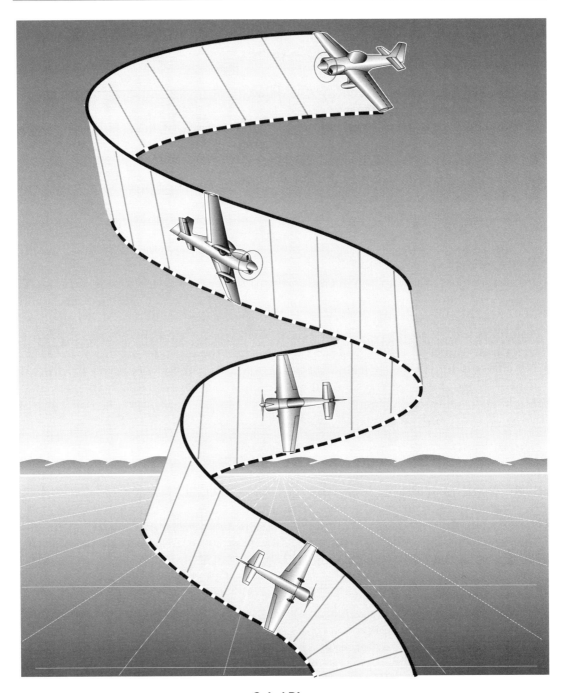

Spiral Dive

The bank increases, the turn tightens, the g builds, the noise builds. There are two possibilities:

- The pilot sees the ground as the aircraft comes out of the bottom of the clouds and his knee-jerk reaction is to pull out, hard. This overloads the horizontal stabilizer, which fails downward and, in the subsequent nose-down pitch, the wings fail upward. This is the *graveyard spiral* which, un-recovered, leads to the loss of the aircraft.
- The other outcome is that the pilot levels the wings to horizontal, closes the throttle and gently raises the nose to the level attitude—a non-event if there is a clear horizon. Note that if the spiral is detected early and the throttle is closed, the pilot only has to level the wings. The nose will come up by itself as the wings are rolled to level. Indeed, the pilot may have to hold forward pressure (terrain clearance permitting) to avoid excessive rolling g.

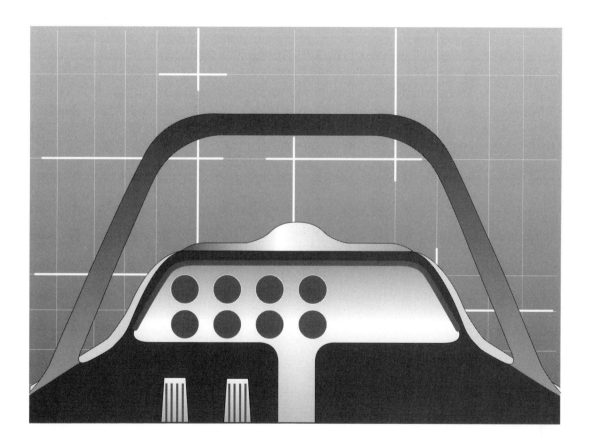

2. The other common scenario is where a pilot is maneuvering in a steep turn and allows the bank angle to increase slightly. If the pilot then increases back pressure to maintain altitude (rather than reducing bank first), the control force tightens the turn rather than raising the nose, and the load factor may become excessive. The nose will drop further and the bank will increase even more. The only recovery is to reduce the bank angle. Again, it is a non-event if there is a clear horizon.

3. The third scenario is during spinning or spin recovery. Some aircraft will not remain in a stable spin unless out-spin aileron is firmly applied throughout. Otherwise the aircraft will slowly accelerate until it is no longer spinning and the nose will drop to a rolling dive (spiral) rather than a true spin. Airspeed and load factor may build quickly. Alternatively, the spin may change to a spiral when spin recovery controls are applied and held—especially if aileron input is also applied. The aircraft may have recovered from stalled flight but the opposite rudder, forward stick and some aileron will cause it to continue to roll, yaw, pitch forward and now accelerate. The increase in airspeed will result in an increase in *g* and in roll and yaw rate. The pilot can now be disorientated especially if he is just recovering from a prolonged spin in the opposite direction and the whole balance mechanism has neutralized to that motion. The tendency is to maintain or centralize the control input. At this stage, the aircraft has a pronounced nose-down attitude, is accelerating, and rolling rapidly. The trim will be tightening the turn. Altitude and time is running out. At least the throttle was left closed—or was it?

In any of these cases, the recovery is very easy, especially if it is initiated early and provided there is a clearly-defined horizon. In small business they say that the three vital requirements for success are, *location, location, location*—provided you start with, *capital, capital, capital*. For aerobatic flight, the three requirements are, *horizon, horizon, horizon*—provided you start with *altitude, altitude, altitude*.

Escape Routes

The Nearest Horizon

You will hear continual reference to the *nearest horizon*. What is it? Simply the horizon which it would take the least pitch to reach. Initially it is easier to explain if we look at an external view of the aircraft then we'll see the corresponding pilot's field–of–view. In this instance, peripheral view is very important. Let's see what we can see.

Clearly inverted:

Erect but steeply, nose down:

Inverted and nose down: the most difficult decision—roll then pull.

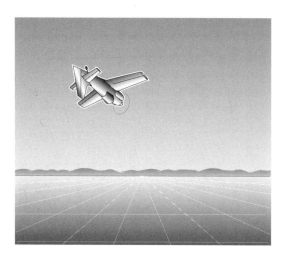 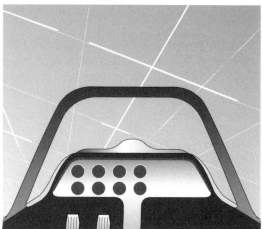

Almost vertical: in which case the visual pattern can be subtle.

 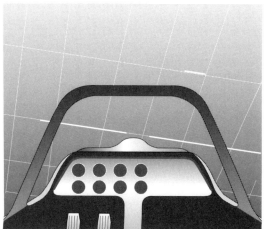

Summary

In most cases, it is safer to roll the airplane until the horizon comes into view and then recover from the dive.

Mishandled or Misjudged Maneuvers

High roll-rate may not seem like a luxury for the more capable aerobatic aircraft and this is certainly true. Unfortunately it is not appreciated how important it can be for pilot survival in any aircraft. The design standards for training aircraft do not place any emphasis on this feature. If ever you get into trouble, safety lies in the ability to quickly regain straight-and-level controlled flight with minimum loss of altitude. This is usually achieved by rolling and then pulling. If the aircraft is sluggish in roll, the aircraft is accelerating and losing altitude and there is little the pilot can do about it. Some proverse rudder may help a little but not much as it cannot generate anything like the rolling power that the ailerons can provide—and you risk a departure.

The answer is not to commit the nose too low if you have any doubt about the clearance. This is especially true of the second half of the barrel roll—as we will discuss later. If in doubt, roll out. Better still, never get into this situation. Some aircraft have a very sluggish rate-of-roll.

Nose-Low Recoveries

A nose-low recovery to controlled flight is simply a sequence which contains the airspeed and allows a gentle recovery to straight-and-level flight without over-stressing the aircraft. It is exactly the same as the spiral dive recovery.

Nose-High Recoveries

A nose-high recovery seeks to avoid a stall and departure from controlled flight. Like any other departure, the immediate actions are to centralize the control column and rudder. Then it remains to simply hold everything (firmly) and then wait until the nose is below the horizon and the aircraft is accelerating. Control the RPM with the throttle.

If the nose-high attitude is not extreme, pushing forward to a level attitude and simultaneously applying full power may recover the situation. However, this is not a comfortable recovery, and if left too late there is a risk of departure with full power applied.

Extreme Attitude and Vertical Recoveries

The importance of containing airspeed
When fully vertical or close to it, there are two short-term concerns and two longer term:
Short-term:
- Avoid any departure by centralizing the controls and closing the throttle.
- Avoid damage to the controls by firmly holding the stick and rudder pedals.
- Then wait for the longer term.
Longer Term:
- Avoid overspeed of the engine by controlling the throttle application.
- Avoid over-stressing the airframe by gently applying *g* as soon as the aircraft is flying and you have a decent horizontal reference, but back-off as the aircraft accelerates.

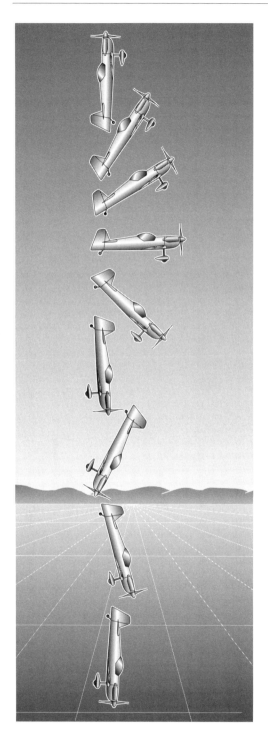

Vertical Recoveries

As soon as there is reversed airflow, caused by backward or tumbling flight, there is risk of airframe damage to the control surfaces, trim tabs, hinges and control linkages.

Vertical recoveries are taught as part of your training because they may be necessary in the event of being hung-up during an attempted Immelmann or other vertical maneuver—even a mishandled loop.

A semi-vertical climb will end in a sudden nose-up (nose-back) or nose-down (nose-forward) pitch (hammerhead) through the vertically down attitude and via a slight oscillation, a vertical dive. This, in itself, is tolerable if the control surfaces are not allowed to move.

Propeller RPM must be contained in the dive by retarding the throttle or applying g as soon as the aircraft accelerates through V_S.

If the climb was truly vertical, the aircraft will slide rearward until the reversed airflow builds in intensity and any slight imbalance in pitching moments causes a violent pitch over through the vertical. If there is a finite delay and the airspeed has built to any degree the reversed airflow can be of such intensity that it can snatch the control column out of the pilot grasp and bang the control surfaces to full deflection. In specially designed aircraft there are control stops to absorb this violence. In most aircraft there are none and permanent damage can result.

Torque effects and the gyroscopic loads on the engine mounts can be considerable.

It is always better to upset a dead vertical position with rudder then centralize and hang on.

Vertical Recovery—Pitching Forward

Tailslides

If the vertical climb is allowed to continue to its logical conclusion, there will be a momentary tailslide and then a violent pitch.

Depending on the exact flight path, the aircraft may pitch forward or backward (backward is more comfortable).

The subsequent flight path and recovery action is similar.

For most situations, it is better to apply and hold rudder deflection to avoid reverse airflow and reverse airspeed building up. If an Immelmann goes awry, centralize the control column, close the throttle and hang on—but keep the rudder applied until the aircraft starts to yaw. It is insurance against the reverse flow.

If the aircraft departs into an incipient spin, then centralize everything.

It is sometimes recommended that the throttle be closed when a vertical recovery is imminent. However, leaving power applied provides the greatest elevator and rudder power and therefore the greatest control. Also, the violence of the pitch is dampened (cushioned) by the airflow.

The RPM has to be controlled when the airplane is accelerating vertically downward.

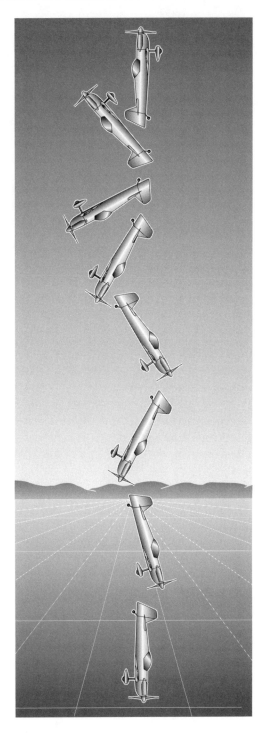

Vertical Recovery—Pitching Back

The Winjeel was an Australian military training aircraft used in the sixties and seventies. (Winjeel is an aboriginal word meaning "little eagle".) It was powered by a 450 hp Pratt and Whitney radial and was a pleasant aerobatic aircraft although it would readily depart from controlled flight if mishandled. It was not unlike a "giant Chipmunk"! It had conventional controls and because of the massive engine, had rudder trim as well as elevator trim.

On Friday afternoons there was no cadet training and the instructors were allocated time to practice their own flying and instructional skills. On one such mutual sortie the instructors were exploring the boundaries of flying skill and decided (before the concept of Cockpit or Crew Resource Management—CRM) if they could work as a crew and fly the aircraft on trim alone—with one instructor handling the elevator trim and the other, the throttle and rudder trim. This proved too easy as they entered turns, climbs and glides.

So they decided a hammerhead would be a more appropriate challenge. The dive and entry was straightforward and as the aircraft reached the vertical position, one instructor was rapidly winding the elevator trim forward from the 3g pull up to maintain the vertical 0g climb and at the appropriate moment, the other wound in full rudder trim. The trim proved insufficient to yaw the aircraft and it started a tailslide. Before the instructors could react, the elevators were violently forced beyond full deflection and the control linkage was broken.

The aircraft completed a natural but violent hammerhead and the instructors were able to recover from the ensuing dive with the elevator trim (the rudder trim having been reset). They successfully returned for a safe landing using the same technique.

So that's the theory of maneuvering flight. Soon it will be put into practice—but first let's look at the effect on the human body and the preparation necessary to carry you safely through aerobatic flight.

Chapter 3

The Physiology of Maneuvering Flight

The human is not designed for the airborne environment. We can, however, be trained and we can, to some extent, become acclimatized.

As humans, we suffer as a result of being designed and evolving to stand vertically erect on the earth, to move slowly and to feel the force of gravity. In flight, the body is subjected to forces and motions which are complex and which can cause the basic earthbound senses to become confused. In most cases, this is not a problem, provided there's a clear visual horizon. With our dominant visual sense, all other inputs are easily overridden and we can virtually ignore other cues.

The process of learning aerobatics, in terms of physiological aspects, is one of acclimating the body to the motions, the rates of yaw, pitch and roll, to load-factors or *g*, and to the confusing sensations caused by simultaneous motions and accelerations in different planes and directions.

In learning aerobatics, we actually go through a process as in learning anything in life, of acquiring a skill and desensitizing those senses which are redundant or not able to accommodate the new motion.

Aerobatic training is also about building an awareness of what to look for, what to expect, what to do about it, and what to do if it goes wrong.

What we call *g* or load-factor, is the total acceleration that both the structure of the aircraft and the pilot's feel during maneuvering flight. It is a combination of a normal force of gravity plus the accelerated loads caused by the changing flight path. Total load factor is the force of gravity plus or minus the applied (additional) load factor.

How an Aircraft Maneuvers

You will recall from Newton's Laws of Motion, that a body wishes to continue in a state of rest or uniform motion in a straight line, unless acted upon by an external force. In the case of our aircraft, the fuselage and its contents, including the pilot, wish to continue in a straight-line at uniform speed. As you know, in normal flight, lift equals weight and even in shallow climb or descent, there's not much difference. If the wings generate two or three times the lift in comparison to the weight, that excess force causes the aircraft to accelerate in the direction of that force.

When an aircraft maneuvers, what happens? The pilot increases the angle-of-attack of the wing and the increased angle-of-attack generates an excess of lift. This excess of lift then changes the flight path of the aircraft.

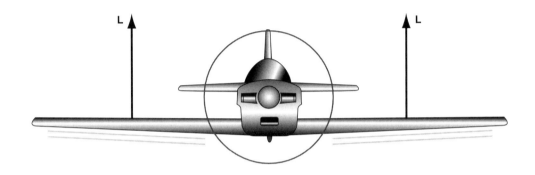

The load is transferred from the wing to the fuselage through the wing-root and struts.

Thus the wings accelerate the fuselage in the direction of the excess lift. The fuselage, through the floor of the cockpit, pushes the pilot's seat upward, the pilot's seat compresses the body from the bottom to the head. (What the pilot feels effectively is that he/she is being squashed down into the seat). In fact, what is happening is that the pilot's seat is squashing his/her spine up toward the head.

When we stand upon the earth, we experience one force of gravity *(g)*. This force of gravity is proportional to the mass of the object and produces the same acceleration for all falling bodies. Therefore as a measure of load factor (force or acceleration), we can use this universal unit of g for any object of any size. In aviation, acceleration is expressed in multiples of the acceleration due to gravity, g (32.2 fps^2 or 9.81 mps^2). If the wings generate twice as much lift (force) as required to balance the weight, then that will accelerate the aircraft in that direction at twice the acceleration due to gravity. The force experienced by the structure and by the pilot is twice the force of gravity or $2g$. If the wing generates three times the lift, then the force felt by the fuselage and the pilot is $3g$, and so on.

Literally the seat pushes toward the pilot's head at two or three times the compression due to normal gravity and we feel the compression of supporting a head and shoulders two or three times its normal weight. It is literally as if you were now carrying two or three heads. As well as the effect on the body's structure or skeleton, it affects everything within the body that has substance or mass. Everything experiences this force.

Physiological Symptoms of Load Factor

We are not designed to be maneuvered. Thus to tolerate forces higher than $+1g$ we have to compensate. The body at $+1g$ can easily function. The heart can pump blood around the total circulatory system, whether it be down to the toes, to the tip of the fingers or up to the head. At $+2g$, literally everything in the pilot's body weighs twice as much as normal, including the blood. As well as overcoming the friction of pumping the blood through what may be partly constricted arteries (or older arteries), the heart has to maneuver blood weighing twice as much to the extremities of the head and the toes. In a standing or sitting position, there's no difficulty getting the blood flow to the feet. However, there is some difficulty getting it back from the feet to the heart. Similarly, the heart has difficulty maintaining blood flow to the head. At $+3g$, the heart has to work three times as hard. At $+4g$, four times. Eventually the eyes and the brain suffer from this reduced blood supply. Vision becomes narrowed, color perception disappears and eventually all vision is lost. There can follow total loss of consciousness.

We can develop our capacity to tolerate g. The body is very adaptable and like most things, it acquires a resistance and an ability to function in unusual situations. The first effect of a reduction of blood supply to the head is on vision and on the brain function. With experience though, a pilot can readily tolerate $4g$ for short periods.

There are physical techniques that you can use, such as tensing the stomach and leg muscles, to help prevent the blood pooling in the lower limbs.

Grey-out, Black-out and *g*-loc

Speed has relatively little effect on the human body, whereas acceleration or deceleration may produce pronounced effects ranging from fatigue to a complete collapse of the cardiovascular system.

The brain and eyes need a continuous supply of oxygen. They have little storage capacity, so strong or prolonged g forces, which reduce the supply, lead progressively to reduced visual acuity, loss of color vision, loss of sight and even unconsciousness. When the acceleration is centripetal, as in turn or pitching maneuver, it is felt by the pilot as an increase in weight. In a 60° level turn, you will experience $2g$, or feel twice as heavy.

As soon as the blood flow to the brain or to the eyes is reduced, then there are physical symptoms. There is some sensation of dizziness or tingling of the brain, the vision becomes focused ahead and we start to lose the peripheral vision. This condition is called *tunnel-vision*. Continuing the g we start to lose color vision, which is called *grey-out*.

Further increasing g forces will lead to total loss of vision, or *black-out*. At this point, the pilot is temporarily blind, though still conscious. Further g increase will inevitably lead to insufficient oxygen and sugar supply to keep the brain functioning and so to *g*-induced loss of consciousness (*g-loc*).

A sequence of sight–related changes occurs before unconsciousness. As these visual symptoms occur while the pilot is conscious, they can be controlled and relieved.

Relaxing the back pressure on the controls will bring nearly-instantaneous relief from the degraded sight condition. The grey-out to black-out phenomena occur so as to act as a warning, a threshold of potential unconsciousness. They are the signal to reduce the control pressure. These symptoms occur at the "normal" rate-of-*g* onset. However, there is appreciable delay before the effects are felt, and there is time to return to normal.

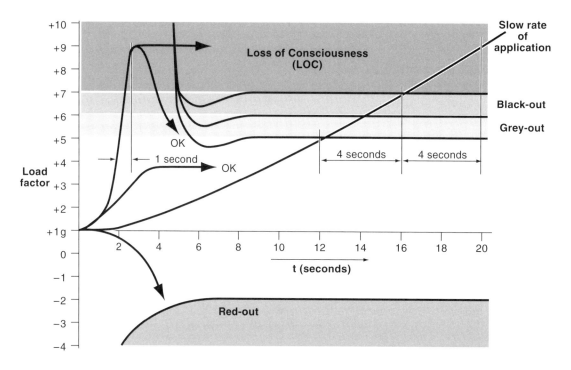

If, however, the rate of application of *g* is rapid, the "warning signals" of degraded sight are bypassed. If the *g* is then sustained, the pilot will become instantly unconscious. If you black out, you will, intuitively, relax the control pressure to reduce the *g* and immediately regain full sight, and you will remain conscious throughout. However, if you lose consciousness, it takes at least 15 seconds to recover. Loss of consciousness is a debilitating experience. (If you have seen someone faint, you will recall how disoriented and incapable they were during the ensuing period.)

A-loc

Another term that has been recently coined is *a-loc*. A-loc is *almost* loss of consciousness due to *g*. The reason for the differentiation is that, even if the pilot does not lose consciousness, there is a temporary period of confusion and even euphoria, where the pilot either does not recognize, or does not care about, the seriousness of the situation. It is momentary but has caused some unexplained pilot lack-of-response during recovery from high-*g* maneuvers.

Recovery

In all cases, if the load factor is removed as soon as the first symptoms appear, the body very quickly recovers to normal. It is only in extremely violent situations, in which the rate of onset of *g* is very high and the *g* is then sustained, that the pilot can momentarily lose consciousness. Even when the *g* factor is removed, there can be a period of confusion. This is believed to have caused several flying display accidents to combat aircraft. For you, *g* will not be a problem. You will build up the aerobatic routine and repertoire of maneuvers slowly and in logical sequence so that initially you only have the mild *g* maneuvers and you will be subjected only to positive *g*. That is, the *g* force retains you in the seat rather than tries to push you out of the seat.

With *g* application, we will also acclimate the body to high rates of onset and high rates of maneuver. These do compound the problem but once again, provided there is a clearly defined horizon and we anticipate the maneuver, the body has no particular difficulty in orienting itself and coping with mild levels of *g*.

Pilot Protection

At load factors much beyond +4*g*, we have to provide assistance to the pilot. You may have heard of *g suits* (or, more correctly, *anti-g* suits) that are worn by fighter pilots. The suit consists of a pair of inflatable trousers, which compress the legs and lower abdomen, thus forcing the blood to remain in the upper body and reducing the pooling in the legs. This considerably assists the heart in maintaining sufficient oxygenated blood to the eyes and brain. Also, we can reduce the vertical distance between legs, head and heart.

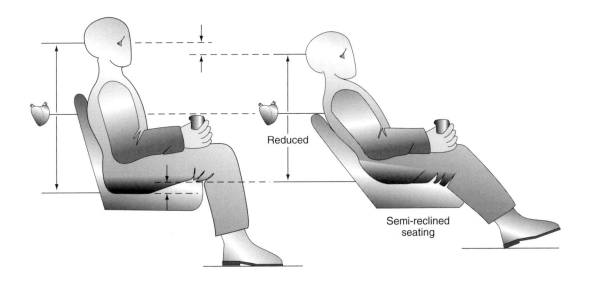

Reduced

Semi-reclined
seating

The famous Focke-Wulf 190 had a second set of rudder pedals above the first, so that for combat (when the brakes were not required!), the pilot legs would be raised to the higher position and thereby reduce the vertical distance from the heart. This reduced pooling of the blood. Many competition aerobatic aircraft also have elevated rudder pedals.

The F16 and competition aerobatic aircraft also have a semi-reclined seating position for the pilot to reduce the vertical displacement of blood from the heart. Inclination is limited by the need to be able to eject and to see.

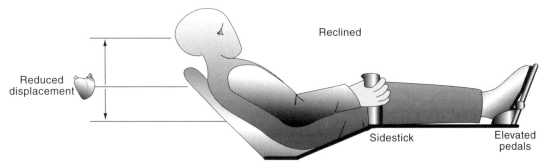

The other factor that affects the body's disability is the duration of the applied load. Most sustained aerobatic maneuvers, such as the loop, take 30 seconds or less and only require +4g. Therefore the amount and the duration of g can be managed. Very high g maneuvers are violent by nature and by necessity of short duration. If you plan an aerobatic sequence so that you have gentle maneuvers in between the high-g maneuvers, then the body can rest and relax and be prepared for the sustained g or for the sudden peak g applications. This is one of the reasons why it is much more difficult to fly as a passenger in aerobatic flight than as the pilot. The pilot knows what's coming next, and so by controlling the rate of application and the duration, the pilot can relax the g when he/she feels symptoms of load factor.

In the fifties, some aircraft were trialed with the pilot in a prone position. But this caused other problems such as the need to support the chin and difficulty in looking over-the-shoulder.

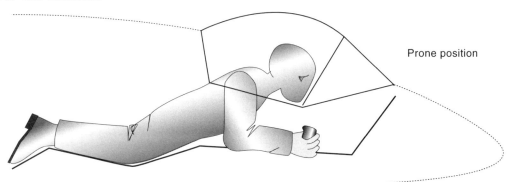

Negative *g*

Negative *g* is the acceleration experienced when the pilot's head is outside the maneuver and thus the blood (and everything else) is forced away from the floor of the cockpit. It is most uncomfortable as the body is supported entirely by the harness and any loose object, including dirt, dust, pencils, coins and mud will float or impact the canopy (unless you have an open cockpit).

Negative *g* maneuvers are really beyond the scope of this book for other than inverted flight (−1*g*). Aside from the discomfort and the feeling of insecurity, one does adapt to quite high levels of negative *g* but these are expert maneuvers in special aircraft.

Symptoms of excessive negative *g* include blood-shot eyes, headaches and even burst blood vessels. Pilots also talk of a condition known as *red-out* where the field-of-view becomes discolored because the lower eye-lid moves over the eye, and there is also excess blood in the eye-ball. With negative *g* there is no *g*-suit protection although semi-reclined seating still helps.

How the Body Senses Motion and Which Way Is Up

Hearing and Balance

Although sight is the most important sense for flying, visual messages to the brain are reinforced or, at times, contradicted by messages from other sensory organs, especially the balance mechanisms in the inner ear (*vestibular* inputs), as well as skin and muscular feeling from all over the body ("seat-of-the-pants" or tactile inputs, known *somatosensory* inputs).

The ear provides two senses—hearing and balance:
- *Hearing* allows you to perceive sounds and to interpret them; and
- *Balance* lets you know which way is up and whether you are accelerating or not. Balance is the next most important sense for a pilot after vision.

Sound is energy that you can detect with your ears. It is often very useful and pleasant, as with voice messages and music, but excessive sound may be annoying and fatiguing, and can even lead to damage within the ear.

Sound signals are caused by pressure waves traveling through the air, and these cause sensitive membranes of the eardrum to oscillate. The inner ear translates these pressure vibrations into electrical signals which are sent via the auditory nerve to the brain where they are interpreted. Sound cues are important to the aerobatic pilot for airspeed and propeller RPM.

Balance and acceleration signals, from the inner ear, pass to the brain as electrical signals for interpretation, but the sensors are designed for a different environment.

The Structure of the Ear

The ear is divided into three areas: the outer, middle, and inner ear.

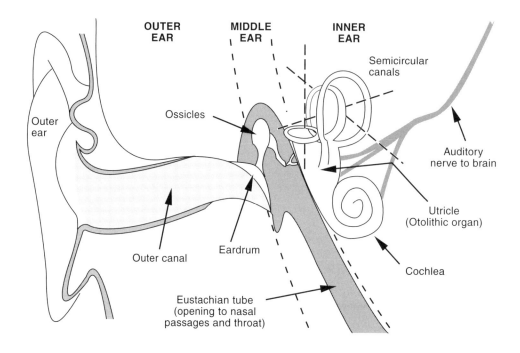

The outer ear includes:
- the external ear (known medically as the *pinna* or *auricle*), which is used to gather the sound signals;
- the outer canal through which the pressure waves pass; and
- the eardrum, which is caused to vibrate in harmony with the pressure waves.

Any obstruction to the outer canal, such as earplugs or an excess of wax, can reduce the sound pressure waves reaching the eardrum. Similarly, a padded cover over the external ear will reduce the sound waves entering the ear.

The middle ear is an air-filled cavity containing three small bones, known as *ossicles,* which are moved by the vibrating eardrum, converting the pressure wave energy into mechanical energy of motion. The ossicles are arranged like a series of levers to increase the effect of the initial movement. This movement then passes on to the cochlea in the inner ear.

The air in the middle ear is maintained at ambient pressure via the *eustachian tube,* which connects the interior of the middle ear to the nasal passages. There is (or should be) no leakage of air across the eardrum, and there should be easy passage of air through the eustachian tube to equalize pressures—for instance, when climbing or descending. (This is sometimes hindered by swelling and inflammation when a person has a cold, and can lead to serious consequences if a person flies with a cold or similar infection.)

Interference to the movement of the three small ossicles or their joints will reduce or distort the sound signal. This can be caused by ear infections, damage to the bones or joints, or a blocked ear with air trapped inside the middle ear *(barotitis)*.

The inner ear contains two very important elements:

- The *cochlea* for hearing; it converts the mechanical energy from the ossicles into electrical signals which then travel via the auditory nerve to the brain for interpretation. Excessive noise can lead to damage of the hairs in the cochlea, and infection or injury can damage the auditory nerve, possibly causing ringing in the ears (tinnitus).
- The *vestibular apparatus* consists of three fluid-filled semicircular canals. Each has a cluster of small hairs at their base. Interaction between the fluid in the canals and the hairs provides sensations of movement—in the three axes of flight—and resulting electrical signals sent to the brain as orientation information. The sensing hairs sit at the base of each semicircular canal in a chamber known as the "cupula." In the same region is the *otolithic* organ (also called the *utricle*), a device which detects linear acceleration or deceleration. It is co-located with, but separate from, the vestibular apparatus.

The ear is never switched-off, and loud or particular noises to which you have a conditioned response can always help stir you from even the deepest sleep. It is interesting to note how you can extract messages of importance to you out of a noisy background—for instance, a radio message directed at you, the sound of your own child on a crowded beach, or your own name mentioned in a distant conversation—known as "the cocktail party effect."

Maneuver Rates

If you rotate a full cup of coffee, you will see that initially, the cup will rotate but the fluid hesitates, until the friction with the walls of the cup causes it to start to move. Eventually, this friction between the coffee molecules will cause the whole contents of the cup to rotate at a uniform speed. If you then stop the cup, the fluid will initially continue at its original speed until friction causes it to slow. A thicker (more viscous), stickier fluid will not hesitate as much. This lag is the means by which the sensors of the inner ear (the semicircular canals) detect radial (rotational) motion and acceleration.

The semicircular canals work in exactly the same way as the cup of coffee.

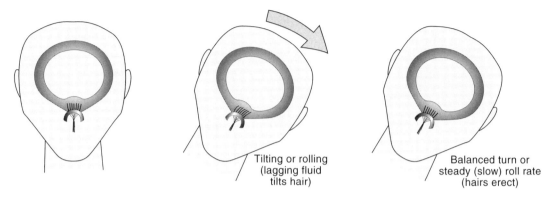

Tilting or rolling
(lagging fluid
tilts hair)

Balanced turn or
steady (slow) roll rate
(hairs erect)

You have three canals—one in each axis so that pitch, roll and yaw are each sensed as a change in relative speed or rest, between the canal and its fluid contents. The change will remain until the body's rotation ceases or becomes steady (that is, no acceleration).

There are also two linear channels—one horizontal and one vertical. These otoliths sense linear speed changes fore-and-aft and up-and-down respectively—like in a lift.

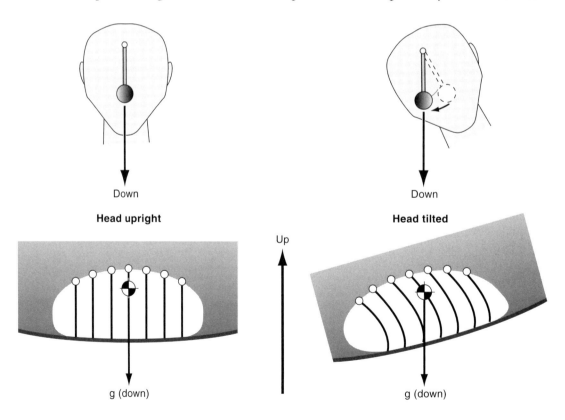

Down

Head upright

Down

Head tilted

Up

g (down)

g (down)

While you have a clearly-defined horizon, there is an over powering order in what you sense. The visual channel keeps you oriented. Other cues either support what you see (and are therefore accepted) or disagree (and are overruled).

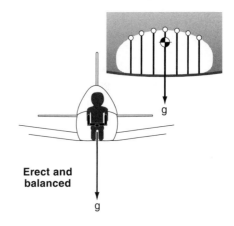

In the absence of a horizon, you rely on the force of gravity as your sense of verticality—modified by any rotational or linear acceleration sensed by the inner ear or the body in general (for example, being pressed into the seat or against the side of the cockpit).

Erect and balanced

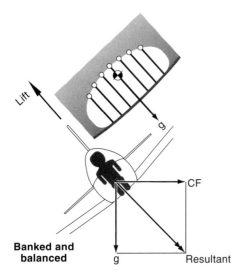

If you add centrifugal reaction caused by maneuvering, as well as the pitch, roll and yaw rates, then the senses have trouble maintaining orientation.

Banked and balanced

Disorientation

Further, beyond four or five continuous rotations the fluids in the inner ear catch up and the sense of acceleration is removed. They now sense no motion. Thus in a sustained spin or a series of consecutive rapid rolls, they are now stable and a spin recovery can actually be wrongly sensed as a spin entry in the opposite direction. The sensation can be sufficiently powerful to cause the pilot to reduce or remove spin recovery controls.

Consecutive, rapid rolls or prolonged spins cause misalignment of the body's senses. It is wise not to enter a high *g* maneuver immediately following rapid rotations. Pause in straight-and-level flight for a few seconds to allow the semicircular fluids to catch up.

Rate of roll alone does not cause as much distress to the body—within the capabilities of normal aerobatic training aircraft unless the rolling is continued through four or five uninterrupted rolls. Competition aircraft, such as the CAP 232 and Sukhoi 31, are capable of very high rates of roll (in excess of 400 degrees-per-second) which if sustained, can actually lead to disorientation, especially if the horizon is less than clearly defined.

The other occasion where you will experience high maneuver rates is in the developed spin. The aircraft is rolling, pitching and yawing and, in some cases, there could be an oscillating motion or rocking. The combination or roll and yaw, especially if the pilot looks ahead at the ground rather than the horizon, can be quite alarming. It is yet another experience for the pilot to accommodate.

If you watch a professional dancer or skater you will notice that, as they spin on the tip of their toes, they watch one point and track it for part of the turn and then quickly pivot their head to regain the same point and once again track it. This prevents dizziness and disorientation. This reference is not available to the pilot; if you imagine the skater spinning with the head aligned to the body and then suddenly stopping, not unexpectedly, they would probably fall over. With high rates of rotation, we are vulnerable to similar disorientation while spinning or rolling. After several turns, the balance mechanism no longer senses the rotation. The eyes have only a blurred view of the earth. When the spin stops, the body is alarmed to sense that it is rotating in the opposite direction (even though it isn't—the stopping is sensed as acceleration in the opposite direction). Thus the pilot is inclined to apply control inputs in the direction of the original spin!

The Body's Ability to Tolerate *g* and Maneuver Rates

Fitness and Recency

A normal, medically and physically fit human can readily adapt to the loads and maneuver rates of a normal aerobatic training aircraft. However, if you take an older body, a less fit body, a body lacking sleep, a body suffering the effect of a hangover or a body that smokes, the tolerance levels are adversely affected.

Tests conducted by the United States Air Force suggest that a moderate, balanced program of aerobics and weight training is best. Extreme aerobic training can actually reduce your tolerance to *g* because of the increased capacity of the blood vessels and lower pulse-rate under stress. Also, recency affects the pilot's ability to cope. Competition and display pilots go through a comprehensive and sustained build-up of both their physical fitness and their aerobatic training to reach the peak values with which they can cope.

To learn aerobatics, and to continue developing, requires the pilot to fly relatively frequently. A gap of even two or three weeks between sorties will show a noticeable reduction in the pilot's capacity to handle *g* and maneuver rates.

It is essential (and common sense) that if you haven't flown for a while, some preliminary time should be spent working-up to the peak g levels and maneuver rates.

An aerobatic training program should bear this in mind and also there should always be a refresher period before embarking on display sequences. If you haven't had the opportunity to fly for several weeks, or maybe even months, then either take the time to slowly work back to the routine, or even carry out a dual sortie with an instructor until you are again up to speed.

Rate of Application/Onset of g

Another consideration with maneuvering is the change of g level. The aircraft structure flexes with the applied load. Flexing is greatest when going from one extreme to the other, so bending of the structure is greatest when going from high negative g values to high positive g and vice versa. Similarly, the body is more stressed by such extremes, for example, from $-1g$ inverted flight to a $+5g$ pull up, and this is when the g-loc phenomenon has most frequently been observed. While it may be less spectacular, it is safer for the aircraft and the pilot to relax the positive or negative g, pause in un-accelerated flight and then apply the next loading. The most dangerous transition is probably from high values of negative g directly to high positive g. A simple solution is to pause in erect $+1g$ flight for a moment to settle down. It is easy to build this into a program.

It is actually possible for the aircraft to be damaged without the pilot feeling the g. A sudden application (called a snatch-pull) which is applied then immediately removed is felt in its entirety by the structure but the body still is settling and accommodating the full load. An instant pull has been known to cause permanent damage to the structure and even in-flight break-up of the aircraft.

Airsickness

Everyone learning aerobatics and spinning will feel uneasy until the body gets to know the motions associated with the different maneuvers. Some aircraft smell of fuel during maneuvers and this aggravates any feeling of sickness. Make sure there is plenty of fresh air and pause between maneuvers. Keep the horizon in sight at all times.

You may feel uneasy when the instructor is flying but most discomfort disappears when you are flying yourself. Most of all, approach the training with a positive attitude. The ill-feeling will pass and you will come to enjoy aerobatics. Many pilots feel no airsickness at all.

Stress and Anxiety

It is normal to feel some apprehension before aerobatic flying. This will diminish with recent and regular practice under the tutelage of a mature, responsible instructor. Stress from daily life is unavoidable and while the advice is to leave it on the ground, it is not always possible. In fact, one of the compelling reasons for aerobatics (or car racing, or rock climbing) is that it requires such total concentration that you are forced to forget other problems. This change of mental focus is as refreshing as sleep.

If you are still feeling anxious about aerobatic flying after several sorties then discuss it openly with your instructor. Stifling anxiety causes it to build up—like the kite rising against the wind. It may be that certain maneuvers or feelings are of concern and they may be rectifiable or avoidable.

Aerobatics in a Hot Climate

The cockpit workload in an aerobatic aircraft is high. It is even more so when you are a beginner. Aerobatic flying in a hot climate is very demanding and it is important to take extra precautions. If it is installed with a canopy, the aerobatic aircraft will have large areas of clear transparency to maximize field-of-view. This means that the cockpit air will heat up quickly in summer. The pilot is also exposed directly to radiant heat and sunburn. It is important to cover the neck, head and forearms. Wear a hat and sunscreen. The fabric or leather flying helmet with built-in headset is good.

Perspiration can be a problem too. A helmet or a headband is useful in keeping sweat out of your eyes. Wear loose-fitting clothes of natural fiber next to the skin. Wash away any gasoline or oil that you may have contacted during the preflight. It will sting when you perspire.

Many aerobatic aircraft are designed in the temperate northern hemisphere and little attention is given to cockpit ventilation for very hot climates. (In some aircraft it is possible to disconnect the heater and use the hot air vents for additional cool air.) Dehydration can be a serious risk. Drink plenty of water and discontinue the sortie if there is any feeling of tiredness, confusion, dizziness or dryness. You may take a water container if it can be stowed safely.

Thermal activity adds difficulty and risk of overstress. Also, summer haze may obscure the horizon. Fly early morning or evening, or choose a higher altitude where haze and thermals are minimized. It is also cooler up there—although maneuver potential is reduced at altitude.

The wearing of parachutes is mandatory in some countries—including the U.S.— but they do add to the potential heat stress. Sheepskin seat covers are a wonderful means of reducing the build-up of perspiration on the back and seat.

Chapter 4

Control Technique and Feel

The most important ability or sensitivity of the skilled aerobatic pilot (or any pilot for that matter) is the feel for the aircraft. Wolfgang Langeweische (*Stick and Rudder*, McGraw-Hill) expressed it beautifully when he referred to the "buoyancy" of the aircraft. This buoyancy or latent ability to maneuver is something a pilot comes to know if he/she flies one aircraft type frequently. It is the potential excess lift, the reserve capacity to instantaneously change flight path, the stored energy, the coiled spring—all of this is buoyancy.

An aircraft at low airspeed is not only sluggish in response, its wing is close to the critical angle-of-attack. It may have plenty of excess thrust but until it actually accelerates to a higher airspeed, it cannot apply even moderate g. Thus it has little ability to maneuver. An aircraft that is also at low altitude has no potential energy to exchange for speed and so is doubly vulnerable. You can study all about the control inputs and speed but the essence of learning aerobatics is the development of this feel for the buoyancy of the aircraft. The essence of finesse is to:

- feel the g;
- feel the onset of buffet;
- feel the floating controls;
- feel the adverse yaw;
- feel the sideslip;
- feel the stick-force lightening;
- listen to the engine;
- hear the airflow and speed; and even
- listen to the silence.

While buoyancy determines your ability to change the flight path, it is excess thrust that allow you to accelerate or to maintain speed at high climb angles or high angles-of-attack.

You have no indication of the lift potential (unless you have an angle-of-attack indicator which shows how much "spare" angle-of-attack you have available at any time), but you do have a crude indication of potential excess thrust just by seeing how much MAP and/or RPM are set compared to the maximum allowable or the maximum continuous—as the case may be. However, you don't want to be looking inside. You need to develop another sensitivity—to the sound of the engine, the sound of the airflow and the position of the throttle lever relative to fully forward and to fully closed. You can develop a similar sensitivity to the position of the stick in relation to the fully forward or fully rearward position—it is the "thermometer" (yardstick) of our buoyancy.

Maneuvering on the buffet is a valuable exercise in learning the symptoms of your aircraft at high angles-of-attack. From normal cruise speed at maximum continuous power, enter a steep turn and tighten until there is stall warning or preferably aerodynamic buffet. Obviously, induced drag increases at this time. Hold the back pressure to keep the buffet and prevent any further speed decay by increasing bank and letting the nose lower. Fly on the edge of the buffet playing bank angle against airspeed. Roll out and reverse the turn or maintain the slight buffet and reverse the turn direction if you have enough energy. It's a terrific way of developing sensitivity to the highest lift potential your aircraft can offer.

The wonderful old Vampire had a subtle *burble* or weak buffet before the drag increased significantly. You could maneuver the aircraft keeping it on the burble and so achieve the absolute maximum turning performance at any speed.

Energy Management

The secret of success for aerobatic maneuvering is managing the energy of the aircraft. If the aircraft slows, you need to apply power to offset the increase in induced drag to avoid continuing to decelerate until the point of stalling. Similarly, if you wish to apply +3 or 4g to enter a loop, you also have to balance the same increase in induced drag by an increase in thrust. As the nose drops or the g is relaxed and the aircraft accelerates, you have to reduce thrust to avoid exceeding limiting speeds or engine RPM. It is the mark of a good pilot, aerobatic or otherwise, that all the time he's/she's making control inputs to maneuver the aircraft, he's/she's making equivalent thrust changes to manage the energy through the flight profile.

Altitude is stored energy. Fighters never engage unless they have an altitude advantage or excess speed (zoom potential)—aerobatics is no different.

Taking into account the performance of the aircraft type requires sensitivity and planning. A series of continuous loops will consume energy quickly. Not using full power when the nose is above the horizon wastes potential altitude gain and therefore potential energy. Not applying full power in anticipation of high g, high alpha and high drag, unnecessarily decays airspeed.

What Does All This Mean?

When planning a maneuver, allow for altitude to convert into entry speed. Allow the aircraft to accelerate to entry speed quickly by avoiding excessive g in the preceding turn or wing-over. Apply full power smoothly as soon as you apply g and at about the same rate. Apply g smoothly and avoid any sign of buffet—that is, relax the g a little if you feel stick lightening or buffet. Apply aileron smoothly but not suddenly, even when you need full deflection.

Where to Look—Leading With Your Chin

A useful practice is to always direct your attention, eyes and head in the direction you wish to go. Staying *ahead* of the aircraft in this way prepares the whole body for the following maneuver. Look for the next horizon (in the direction you will be going) and also try to keep part of the aircraft structure within your field of view. The eyes lead and look out, the head follows, then the hands and feet move the controls. The aircraft responds and the eyes and other senses check the response of the aircraft—and make adjustments if necessary. Watch a dancer or gymnast.

When planning a sequence, plan low-*g* maneuvers, such as wing-overs and hammerheads, in between high-*g* maneuvers and use the thrust and upward momentum in these vertical maneuvers to maximize altitude gain and minimize altitude loss—that is, nose up, full power—nose down, reduce power (unless applying *g).*

Technique

The technique for various aerobatic maneuvers has to be modified to suit the aircraft type and its limitations—whether system or performance. It's just like the over-taking maneuver in a car. If you have plenty of excess power then the maneuver is not critical. If you are in an under-powered vehicle passing a truck on a hill then the maneuver requires judgment and timing to build up excess energy and pull out at the right time and you need an escape route!

For example, basic aerobatic aircraft (called *limited aerobatic, semi-aerobatic* or *utility category,* as distinct from, *fully aerobatic*) are typically limited in excess thrust and control response as well as ultimate load factor. Such aircraft are not capable of all maneuvers and suffer reduced performance to the extent that special techniques have to be employed.

An aircraft such as a Chipmunk or Cessna Aerobat has to be climbed to a start point sufficient to allow a progressive loss of altitude throughout the maneuvers or sequence. Several aircraft, even with 450 hp, have to be climbed to nearly 10,000 feet to allow a ten-minute aerobatic sequence.

The maneuvers themselves must be adjusted also.

- If the engine has no collector tank for limited inverted flight, the engine would cut from fuel starvation as soon as negative *g* was sustained. (If it didn't cut, the engine would soon be starved of oil anyway.) To perform a slow roll in this aircraft you would have to be ready for an engine cut halfway through and close the throttle so that the engine didn't over-speed when the fuel supply returned. A float type carburetor would cut the fuel supply to the engine as soon as positive *g* was removed. Also there is a danger of stalling if the pilot tries to sustain inverted level flight with the engine stopping.
- An Immelmann would require a steep dive, very high entry speed and loss of altitude, a high-*g* pull up and a downward path to allow an aileron roll to level-flight without having to sustain negative *g.*

- Aircraft with a limited inverted fuel supply would then be limited by a loss of oil pressure after 30 seconds or so of inverted flight or when the oil pressure dropped suddenly. Inverted flight is difficult enough without having to monitor the oil pressure gauge. Getting to know the aircraft and counting a safe number of seconds is easier than monitoring instruments.
- Induced drag also plays an important role. An aircraft with straight wings, high wing loading and low aspect ratio (therefore the span loading is high, that is, the weight is carried over a small wingspan) and large square wingtips, may be fast but would lose performance when maneuvering at high angles-of-attack.
- Aircraft with a high wing or longer span tend to have a reduced rate-of-roll. Incidentally, the restricted rate-of-roll is a major limitation in being able to escape from a mishandled maneuver. For example, if the nose is allowed to drop too far during the second half of a barrel roll then the only recovery is to roll to the nearest horizon and pull out. People who have rolled large transport aircraft carried this enormous risk as they were unable to quickly roll to level and may not have been able to generate enough drag to contain the dangerous build-up of airspeed. Imagine if the nose of the Boeing 707 had dropped during the second half of the barrel roll.
- Aircraft with cambered airfoils and positive angle-of-incidence require a large attitude change and a pronounced forward stick position to maintain level inverted flight. Many basic aerobatic trainers have limited forward stick available for negative *g* maneuvers and outside turns. Power and airspeed need to be maintained to be able to hold the inverted position.
- Aircraft with dihedral are less stable in inverted flight so more effort is required to keep the wings level and the aircraft balanced.

Don't be deterred by any of this. It simply requires that the type of maneuver and the technique for each is adjusted to suit the capabilities of the aircraft—as they should be—and the type of aircraft is chosen to suit the style of the individual pilots.

The Use of Trim

As discussed, the essence of aerobatic flying and energy management is developing a feel for the onset of buffet, being aware of stick force and position as a guide to an impending stall, and noticing control loads and wind noise as a guide to engine RPM and airspeed.

The development of this sensitivity is adversely affected if the aircraft is constantly retrimmed to remove out-of-trim stick forces. As a general rule, most properly designed aerobatic aircraft have only a small trim change with changing airspeed so that the out-of-trim forces are not excessive over the operating envelope of the aircraft. In this case, it is preferable to trim the aircraft at an airspeed corresponding to cruise at maximum continuous power and leave it set.

Any reduced airspeed (increased angle-of-attack) will be reflected in the necessary pull-force. Similarly, speeds above this will be indicated by the push-force required. Trim (out-of-trim force) is a very valuable reference for flying by feel and, therefore, for developing a sensitivity for aerobatic maneuvering. With this feel, you can also spend more time looking outside. You are flying by instinct rather than flying by numbers.

The Use of Power

Power Control and Care of the Engine

Fixed-Pitch Propeller
Engine handling with a fixed-pitch propeller is crucial to avoiding an RPM overspeed on the downward-side of maneuvers—especially the loop, hammerhead and perhaps the barrel roll. The RPM increase is the result of a high power throttle position and increasing airspeed. The RPM can be contained in one of two ways:
• by retarding the throttle; or
• by applying *g* and using the increased induced drag to contain the airspeed increase.
  Some aircraft are more prone to overspeed than others. You will become familiar with the precautions needed for your aircraft.

Constant-Speed Propeller
The constant-speed propeller is far less prone to overspeed, although it can happen. When increasing the power too suddenly while the airspeed is increasing rapidly and there is no aerodynamic resistance to high RPM, the governor may not prevent the RPM limit being exceeded. Avoiding the momentary overspeed simply requires normal restraint on the rate of throttle increase.

  Also a loss of oil pressure (for example, when the engine stops or when inverted behind the limits of the oil system) reduces the control of the governor and an overspeed can result. For this reason, some aerobatic aircraft have a special propeller which moves to full coarse pitch (lowest RPM) when the oil pressure drops—thereby preventing an overspeed.

Torque and Slipstream
As well as managing energy, the use of power has an enormous effect on controllability at low airspeeds. We are used to high airspeed with stiff controls and high *g*. We are used to low airspeed with light controls and low *g*. Now we need to consider the unusual combination of low speed, sloppy ailerons, high power, powerful elevators and rudder, high torque, high yawing moments, all in an aircraft with relaxed stability (so that it is highly maneuverable).

  When we are considering low airspeed, we are now talking of airspeeds at and well below the stalling speed of the aircraft. How so?

The stalling speed is the speed in level flight at which the airfoil reaches its critical angle-of-attack—its stalling angle. Stalling speed is determined by a particular aircraft's weight, power and configuration. If we are not in level flight, the angle-of-attack can be anything we make it. We can reach the stalling angle at twice the stalling speed by applying $4g$. Conversely, we can fly at half the stalling speed and stay below the critical angle-of-attack if we are maintaining less than $1g$. At $+0.5g$ (½ weight so ½ lift required) we can fly at ¼ of the stalling speed (V_2) and we still won't stall the wing. At $0g$ we won't stall at all—even at zero airspeed. However, all of these situations involve a changing flight path and are transitory. We can't return to $1g$ flight until the airspeed is back above V_S and we must have sufficient altitude to enable this to happen—for the aircraft to accelerate and then apply g to recover from the dive.

Let's look at a practical example. An aircraft such as the Pitts Special is able to roll around a vertical flight path and rotate in roll at zero airspeed due to the torque reaction of its relatively powerful engine. At zero forward speed there is little aerodynamic resistance to yawing. It can pause at the top of a vertical climb and can rotate in yaw because of the powerful slipstream effect over the rudder and the low directional stability.

Engine Stoppage and Restart

In many aircraft, especially with fixed-pitch propellers, the engine may stop due to reversed airflow in hammerheads and tailslides. Some will stop in a spin. Many have limited inverted flight time before the engine will stop due to interruption of fuel supply or loss of oil pressure. It is not a serious problem.

If the engine stops, close the throttle so there is no risk of overspeed when it restarts. If the engine does not start as the aircraft accelerates, or if the propeller remains stationary (some aircraft require a very steep dive before it will begin rotating), continue diving as altitude permits. The Tiger Moth needs an almost vertical dive. If a dive doesn't start it rotating, then simply engage the starter (with the throttle closed). The rotation will bring the propeller blades into a positive angle-of-attack, and the engine will quickly restart. Then check for throttle response — after you recover from the dive.

Slipperiness

Most of the aircraft we fly at training schools are *draggy* with a fixed landing gear and perhaps external bracing. The newer generation of composite structure, high-performance aircraft are another ball game. They are slippery (aerodynamically clean) with retractable gear and they are highly powered. They are stressed for aerobatics but there is no trainer. Converting to one of these types is as significant a step as the initial aerobatic training. Type-specific training is essential for these aircraft.

Chapter 5

Preparing for Aerobatics

When you decide to learn aerobatics, approach it like any other training course and consider all aspects, including cost.

Don't accept an invitation from a friend to show you how it's done—not a single maneuver. Go with a qualified and current instructor, in an approved aircraft, at a safe altitude, with proper preparation and briefing. Accept nothing less. So many pilots and passengers have refused to fly again or to learn aerobatics because they have had a scary experience with an inexperienced pilot showing off.

Attend an organized training curriculum and fly frequently until the maneuvers become almost second nature.

How to Learn

Choosing an Aerobatic Trainer

What makes an airplane aerobatic? An airplane must be designed specifically for aerobatic flight. It has greater structural strength than a *normal* category airplane, it has been tested for acceptable control response and spin recovery characteristics and has an emergency in-flight egress facility. It may be approved for limited maneuvers in the *utility* category, which requires the plane to be loaded within special limits, or it may be fully aerobatic and have special systems for aerobatic flight, for inverted flight and for display flying.

Design Features

The aerodynamic features of an aerobatic aircraft were covered in chapter 2. For training, your choice may be limited. For initial training and for carrying a passenger, it is comforting to have a side-by-side seating arrangement. For progression to club or competition aerobatics or formation flying, the tandem configuration is better. For other than the very basic positive *g* maneuvers, choose an aircraft that offers at least a limited time inverted.

There are many advantages to choosing an aircraft with control columns (joy-sticks) rather than the control wheel. The stick operates in the logical sense in all directions whereas the yoke has to be rotated. The stick is more directly geared and you can exert more direct force, more quickly. The stick leverage allows better control. The hand can be rested on the thigh during high *g* maneuvers so they are less tiring. The hand does not slip and there is less tendency to apply aileron under *g* as there is with a yoke.

It is important to fly with one hand on the control column and the other on the throttle. There are occasions when the power has to be quickly applied or removed. Having said that, some aircraft do sometimes require the strength of both hands to achieve full control deflection.

An aircraft with a constant-speed propeller is much easier to manage than a fixed-pitch propeller which tends to overspeed in some maneuvers. An aircraft with a throttle quadrant allows the hand to be rested on a firm surface under high g so there is no tendency for the hand to drop off the lever—and with support for the hand, it is possible to make more subtle changes than with the unsupported, plunger-type throttle.

A low-wing or mid-wing aircraft will offer a better field-of-view when maneuvering and probably offer a higher rate-of-roll. Biplanes offer advantages and disadvantages, depending on their airfoils, controls and power. A Pitts Special is very different from a Waco.

Most aerobatic aircraft have a tailwheel configuration and fixed landing gear. It should have two accelerometers—one of which should not be resettable (alternatively, it should have an electronic flight recorder). Choose an aircraft that is comparable in handling and performance to the one you will fly later. If you have a high performance sports aircraft which is "slippery," there is little point training in a Tiger Moth or a Stearman.

Check the cockpit ventilation if you are flying in a hot climate. There is a real risk of heat stress and dehydration. Open cockpits are fun on a warm day.

Aircraft Systems and Limitations

Engine and Propeller
The engine and propeller for basic maneuvers are no different from other GA aircraft. A constant-speed propeller makes it easier for the pilot to control power and to avoid overspeeding the engine. More power allows more maneuvering and less time climbing, but it also means more torque which must be managed.

Oil Systems
An aerobatic aircraft will have time limits on inverted flight and negative g (due to loss of oil pressure and risk of engine damage) unless there is an inverted oil system. This system continues to supply oil under pressure even with negative g.

Fuel Systems
The float type carburetor will stop feeding fuel under negative g and the fuel lines from the tank also start to suck air. Therefore, a utility category airplane is usually restricted to positive g maneuvers. Some aircraft have a separate fuel reservoir within the main fuel tank for a limited endurance under negative g—perhaps thirty seconds or so. A pressurized fuel-injection system is used for aerobatic aircraft.

Smoke Systems

Airplanes that are used for airshows have a smoke system fitted so that the aircraft is more visible and the flight path more obvious. The smoke is generated in one of two ways:

- Light oil or hydraulic fluid is sprayed into the hot engine exhaust which produces a trail of white smoke. This may be colored with dyes. The spray is controlled by a switch or a lever in the cockpit and can be run continuously or at particular times.
- Alternatively, pyrotechnics (smoke grenades) are fitted to the wing-tips and triggered from the cockpit. Once they are ignited, they have to burn out and cannot be controlled.

The cover photo of the French Connection shows both systems in use. The white smoke from the exhaust, and the colored pyrotechnics from the wing-tip flares, are clearly visible.

Emergency Egress and Parachutes

It is an FAA requirement that parachutes are worn, under some circumstances, and that there is a single-action, emergency in-flight egress system. For airplanes with a canopy over the cockpit, this system is usually a means of canopy jettison where the retaining latches are undone and the canopy is carried away by the air loads. For aircraft with a door to the cockpit, the escape system is a handle which removes the hinge pin, and the door is then pushed out.

Ask your instructor for advice on your egress system and the fitting and use of the parachute. Ask to be shown the packing date, how to fit the harness correctly and how to use it. Treat it carefully. Do not use it as a cushion on the ground and don't leave it in the sun. Avoid fuel or oil spills and, if they do occur, have the parachute inspected.

Choosing an Instructor

Attitude is everything. Age does not matter nor does total experience. It is the ability to teach and the ability to demonstrate consistent, safe maneuvers that you are seeking. Find an instructor who loves flying, loves aerobatics, and loves to teach—if you can. They are rare but worth seeking. Contact the International Aerobatic Club at their website and select a qualified and recognized school and instructor.

Choosing a School

The school is less important than the instructor and the aircraft but check how well the training and the maintenance is managed and how they present and care for their aircraft. Choose a school that follows an approved syllabus of training.

Aerobatic Area

No matter how good your look out, you can't adequately cover an area sufficiently well during an aerobatic sequence, especially if you are learning or teaching. If possible, choose a training school which has access to a dedicated aerobatic area—so you know you are the only one in it. There's nothing more disconcerting than meeting another aircraft as you go over the top of a loop or when you are half way though a spin entry.

Self-Evaluation/Preparation

Medical Fitness

Aerobatics can be strenuous. You need a minimum of average medical and physical fitness or you will feel the strain. Don't fly with any illness, no matter how slight—no head-cold, flu symptoms or nausea. Ask your doctor if there is any condition about which you are unsure. Also, if you are using medication, ask about its acceptability for flying.

Don't fly with a hangover—ever. It lowers your tolerance to *g*, to roll rates, to disorientation and to dizziness. It affects your mental processing speed and your ability to concentrate. It also leaves you dehydrated, unrested and unrefreshed—and it's no fun.

Physical Fitness

You don't need to be an athlete for aerobatics—at least not until you reach the competitive stage. At the beginning, normal fitness is fine but fresh air and regular exercise will sharpen your senses, brain function and tolerance to *g*. I believe Ayrton Senna once said, *"the best exercise for Grand Prix drivers is Grand Prix driving."* It's the same with aerobatics. The maneuvers themselves, regularly practiced, provide aerobatic exercise for the total mind and body. Having said that, moderate aerobic exercise improves alertness, tolerance to *g*, self esteem and the ability to learn. What more can I say?

Hardening

The best way to build a tolerance to aerobatic maneuvers is to do aerobatics. There is no other way to replicate the stress, *g*, roll rates, vibrations, sensations and visual cues.

Sleep and Diet

Fly only after normal rest. Aerobatics after a late-night (or early-morning) party are not fun. Before flying, eat a light breakfast and avoid greasy food—until you are acclimated to aerobatics. Toast or cereal is good. Energy foods such as muesli bars and carbohydrates are also good. You will be burning energy. Some people like fruit and yogurt but some find it unsettling. You know yourself. Drink plenty of water—not too much coffee.

Mental Preparation

Read about flying and aerobatics. Sit in the aircraft and imagine the maneuvers—especially after the first lesson. Be able to quickly read the airspeed, altitude and *g*.

Once you have established a basic sequence, rehearse it in your mind regularly, down to the smallest detail of where you are going to look, what power you are going to set and what entry speeds you will be looking for. Try to do it in real time—that is, the rate at which it will actually happen in flight. Alan Jones, the Australian world driving champion, rehearsed so well that when he was actually racing, it was like he was observing his body driving the car and he was able to concentrate on tactics and assessing the track— *"looking through the window of his helmet,"* was how he described it.

Competition pilots do a *rain dance*. They walk through the maneuvers as they rehearse their sequences on the ground. Learn speeds, power settings, attitudes and limitations by heart. A cue card is okay between sequences, but it's far better to learn the routine by heart like a choreographed dance routine. Imagine Nureyev reading his ballet steps from a card. Aerobatic routines, even basic ones, are no different.

Emergency procedures should be practiced until they are automatic. Escape/egress procedures should be demonstrated and practiced if you are going to wear a parachute. Ask your instructor about bailing out during a spin.

Recency (How Often You Fly)

When planning your program, try to arrange your time and resources so you can fly regularly and fairly frequently. The ideal is to take a continuous period of a week or so and fly every day. Once you complete your initial training, maintain recency by flying your routine at least every month or so—more frequently for advanced sequences. If you cannot fly for an extended period, then return to aerobatic flying incrementally—that is a flight of wing-overs, steep turns and stalls, then basic maneuvers before returning to a sequence. If the period is prolonged, then the safe option is to fly with a safety pilot (an aerobatic instructor) for the first sortie and refresh any aspect about which you are uncertain. Even a ground briefing helps considerably. Know the *HASELL* checks:

H	Height	sufficient to recover by 1,500 feet AGL—or as approved.
A	Airframe	landing gear, flaps—as required—trim for max cruise IAS.
S	Security	harness tight, headset secure, no loose objects, no sharp objects.
E	Engine	fuel on and contents, boost pump on, carb heat cold, mixture, set max continuous rpm.
L	Location	not over built-up area, not over clouds, not over water, clearly defined horizon, note sun position, note direction to home or landing area, clearance or clear of Controlled Airspace. Pick prominent features and be within gliding distance of a suitable landing field.
L	Look Out	wing-overs and clearing turns as required. Check your blind spots.

- Check whether your aircraft requires carb heat for stalling and spinning practice.
- Recall the aircraft's recommended speeds and any applicable limitations.
- Recall the maneuvers and your flight sequence.

Clothing

Flying Suit

It is more comfortable to wear a flying suit or clothing without a tight waist band. Also, the flying suit allows you to safely stow pencils, keys, etc. (which really would be better left on the ground). Underclothing should be comfortable and of natural fiber. Be careful to avoid fuel spills on your clothes during the preflight. It seriously irritates the skin when you perspire. The smell during flight is also unsettling.

Shoes

Soft flexible shoes, with no tread, are preferable. Tread picks up stones from the tarmac and also can restrict movement of the feet over the floor of the cockpit when applying full rudder.

Gloves

Gloves are valuable as they grip the plastic of the controls and trim wheel. Your hands will also be sweaty and slippery.

Scarf/Headband

It is very handy to have a sweat band or a cotton scarf that you can use to wipe your forehead and eyes—alternatively you may use the fabric back of the gloves.

Headset Security

A fabric or leather helmet keeps the earphones in place and also captures sweat. Alternatively, a cat's collar (it has an elasticized segment) can be attached to a normal headset and functions well as a chin-strap. Route the headset lead through your harness to avoid interference with the controls.

Hats and Sunscreen

The effects of radiation should not be underestimated. Wear a soft hat and sunscreen—but keep it away from your eyes. Fly early morning or late evening in summer.

Sunglasses

Glare can be distracting. Quality sunglasses are invaluable to remove glare and to improve visibility. Ensure they are properly restrained and that the frames do not significantly interfere with your field-of-view.

Secure the glasses with an elastic headband or attach them to the headset frame. Alternatively, for those of us who wear corrective lenses, an additional set of anti-glare goggles with a headband can be attached over the top of standard glasses and without interfering with the field-of-view.

Preflight Inspection

Be very thorough with all preflight inspections—a training aircraft is exposed to a harsh environment.

Loose Objects

Don't add to the collection by carrying pens, pencils and coins into the aircraft. It is amazing how many aircraft have been lost due to jammed controls arising from a misplaced loose object.

If you drop something, discontinue aerobatics until you locate it.

If the aircraft has undergone maintenance, be doubly careful to inspect the cockpit and rear fuselage. Tools could have been left inside. If you perform maintenance on an aerobatic aircraft, please account for all tools before signing-off the work.

Kneepad Security

Use a soft kneepad and make sure that it is secure and does not restrict full and free movement of the control column.

Strapping-In

Aerobatic aircraft will have a four- or five-point harness, perhaps also with an additional lap-strap.

The five-point harness should be locked and tightened as follows:

- Loosen all straps.
- Close and lock the buckle.
- Tighten the lap-straps so they press down and retain the pelvis above the hip joint. This ensures the skeleton is firmly attached to the aircraft.
- Tighten the crotch strap and tuck away the loose end under your thigh.
- Tighten the shoulder straps to remove any slack but not so tight that you cannot swivel your head and shoulders. You should be able to see the vertical stabilizer out of the corner of your eye. Ensure that the control column is free and that it won't unlatch the lever of the lap buckle.
- Attach and adjust the additional lap-strap harness.

Some higher performance aircraft even have a ratchet on the harness to securely hold the lower abdomen. Some have double lap-straps. Some aircraft also have a negative-g strap on the rudder pedals or even ski-boot type attachments to retain the feet during negative-g maneuvers.

Fit the helmet or headset and connect the lead. Try to route it so that it will not float around during maneuvers and cannot interfere with the control column. Stow any loose objects.

FAA Regulations

There is no formal requirement for an endorsement or rating to fly aerobatic maneuvers. However, the most important aspect is to receive proper training from a qualified and responsible person.

The aircraft must be approved and correctly loaded for both weight and balance. You may need to wear a parachute. You must be clear of other traffic and not in controlled airspace. You must maintain a safe altitude.

For display flying, you may gain a waiver from the FAA, and you may gain special approval for low-level aerobatics under the Aerobatic Competency Evaluation program (ACE). Talk to other aerobatic pilots and visit the websites of the International Aerobatic Club (IAC) and the Experimental Aircraft Association (EAA) for a chapter in your state.

Regulations Governing Aerobatics

The FAA defines "aerobatic flight" as an intentional maneuver involving an abrupt change in an aircraft's attitude, an abnormal attitude, or abnormal acceleration, not necessary for normal flight. The FAA defines an aerobatic maneuver as one which has:
- a bank of 60° relative to the horizon; or
- a nose-up or nose-down attitude of 30° relative to the horizon.

Aerobatics may not be performed in a careless or reckless manner so as to endanger the life or property of another. Additionally, aerobatic flight may not be conducted over the following areas:
- any congested area of a city, town or settlement;
- over an open air assembly of persons;
- within the lateral boundaries of the surface areas of Class B, Class C, Class D, or Class E airspace designated for an airport;
- within 4 nautical miles of the center line of any Federal airway;
- below an altitude of 1,500 feet above the surface;
- or when flight visibility is less than 3 statute miles.

The airspace utilized for aerobatics should be carefully selected. You should avoid known student training areas, military low level routes, approach paths, nearby airports (unless specifically authorized), and any other areas known to be congested with itinerant traffic.

All U.S. military pilot training courses include aerobatic flight. The purpose of this training is to instill confidence in the pilot's ability to handle the aircraft and perform precision maneuvers in all flight attitude regimes, as well as recover from extreme attitudes. The FAA does not require the performance of "pure" aerobatic maneuvers during any civilian flight tests, other than the spin requirement for airplane flight instructor applicants. Therefore, the FAA has not been involved in establishing criteria for the performance of aerobatic maneuvers or the certification of flight instructors to teach aerobatics.

However, they recognize the value of aerobatics in pilot training and encourage all pilots to seek out training with an experienced aerobatics instructor. The FAA does not regulate the contents of an aerobatic training curriculum, but pilots are encouraged to seek out a school that uses a structured syllabus such as the one you'll find in chapter 8 of this book.

Be sure your aircraft is certificated in the *aerobatic* category before beginning any aerobatic maneuvers. However, the aerobatic category does not mean that all aerobatic maneuvers can be flown. Operating limitations must be observed. The difference between aerobatic category aircraft and *normal* or *utility* is basically the limit load factors, or *g* forces the structure can withstand. Naturally, aerobatic aircraft must be built stronger. Maneuvers that can be performed safely are listed either in the approved aircraft flight manual or on placards located in the cockpit. Safe entry speeds are also listed. These limitations must be closely observed. All of the other limitations should be followed as well, such as airspeed, rpm, temperature, and other maximums.

Pay particular attention to the weight and balance, as many aerobatic aircraft have lower gross weight requirements for performing aerobatic flight, and be careful to account for the additional weight of any parachutes. Also, the CG position is critical to stability and control characteristics as well as spin recovery.

Familiarize yourself with the unique characteristics of the aerobatic aircraft. Be sure to study the airplane's flight manual and know it well.

Whenever you carry a passenger, you may not exceed 60° of bank or 30° of pitch up or pitch down unless both occupants wear an approved parachute. (You do not have to wear a parachute when you fly alone.)

Waivers

A *Waiver* is an official document issued by the FAA which authorizes certain deviations from the regulations, but under conditions that maintain an equivalent level of safety. Waivers are issued for the purpose of aviation events or aerial demonstrations, to include airshows, aerobatic contests, and practice areas designated for aerobatic proficiency or training. For purposes of an aviation event, an aerobatic maneuver means an intentional maneuver in which the aircraft is in sustained inverted flight or is rolled from upright to inverted or from inverted to upright position. All standard aviation event aerobatic maneuvers, such as slow rolls, snap rolls, loops, Immelmanns, Cuban eights, spins, hammerhead turns, etc., may not be performed over congested areas or over spectators. Waivers vary to suit the requirements.

Some events require nothing more than waiving the regulation to permit aerobatic flight at less than 1,500 feet above the surface. Others may require waiving aircraft speed limitations, minimum safe altitudes, or limitations while operating in the vicinity of airports. Visit your local FAA Flight Standards District Office (FSDO) for FAA Form 7711-2, Application for Certificate of Waiver or Authorization, which is used when applying for FAA Form 7711-1, Certificate of Waiver or Authorization.

Preparatory Flying

Before attempting any new maneuvers, refresh your visual flying technique. Start with steep turns, stalls, high and low speed handling and visual look out. Refresh the attitudes and power settings for the various flight paths. Nominate entry speeds and use a feature on the horizon or a line feature on the ground to position and align the aircraft. Discipline yourself to fly as accurately as you can. Start to plan ahead, i.e. as you complete one maneuver already have a plan for the next maneuver and the entry conditions that you want.

Anticipate the flight path of the aircraft, and have your head and eyes looking ahead, continuously comparing attitude and direction, airspeed and altitude. Fly from a climb to a glide, to a climb, to a climbing turn, to a level steep turn, to slow flight, to a stall — controlling attitude, airspeed and power as you do so and keeping the aircraft balanced. It's a very good exercise.

Develop a continuous visual scan cycle of *attitude, position and direction, instruments, lookout, instruments, attitude, position and direction, etc.*

If you are flying a new aircraft type, then spend some time getting to know it. Also, get to know the prominent features in your area and have some to use for orientation and position. Look for suitable forced landing fields—just in case.

If you have flown recently and a sensible, progressive aerobatic training program is being followed, you will have no problem with disorientation. Always insist on a clearly defined horizon and stay well clear of clouds. Start at a safe altitude. If you do "lose the place" during maneuvers, roll to the nearest horizon, and settle down for a while in straight-and-level flight. Allow your personal gyroscope to re-erect itself.

Chapter 6

Aerobatic Maneuvers

You can't learn how to fly from a book but you can learn what to expect, what to avoid and how best to prepare. As a result, your airborne time will be more productive and your retention of training will be improved. Armchair aerobatics can be very valuable. Let's imagine a basic course in aerobatics and consider some of the more important aspects of each of the maneuvers. We'll start at the beginning with steep turns.

Maximum Performance Turning

A maximum performance turn on the buffet, playing bank against pitch attitude and thrust against airspeed, is an art and a quality that an aerobatic pilot must acquire (in fact, *all* pilots should acquire).

Description

Maximum performance turning is the ability to maneuver in the most efficient way at any speed. It requires the anticipation to increase thrust as g is applied, to be sensitive to stall warning cues, and to be able to sustain the aircraft at the point of buffet. At this stage the pilot should be able to look outside the aircraft and adjust the pitch attitude by maintaining back pressure and temporarily adjusting the bank.

Piloting Technique

Set maximum continuous power and trim the aircraft in straight-and-level flight. Roll into the turn (aileron and rudder) and apply full power. Increase the back pressure and bank angle slowly. Cross-check the attitude and the airspeed until the aircraft is maintaining airspeed at the point of buffet. Note this attitude, speed and load factor. Raise the nose attitude by reducing bank, and allow the airspeed to reduce. Reduce back pressure to maintain the buffet short of the stall. Increase the bank,

Attitude in a Steep Turn

lower the nose and allow the airspeed to increase. Increase the back pressure to maintain the buffet until you are back to the attitude and speed with which you began.

Points of Airmanship

Keep looking outside with only brief looks at the ASI, altimeter and accelerometer.

Wing-Over

Description

The wing-over is a very easy maneuver to perform but a very difficult maneuver to define in that it can be almost anything you want it to be.

It can be a climbing maneuver, a descending maneuver, a turning maneuver, a tight maneuver or a loose maneuver; it can have high bank angle, low bank angle, high *g*, low *g*, high power or low power.

Begin with a set-piece wing-over, through 90° and then 180°, both to feel the characteristics of the aircraft and also to learn where to look and when to look—for what references. Having mastered this, you will then use a variety of wing-overs to align the aircraft with a ground reference and to set the attitude and airspeed for entry into the next aerobatic maneuver.

The wing-over is the easiest, most pleasant, and most useful maneuver. It is taught to pilots as an escape maneuver, in a blind valley, but it is dangerous near the ground.

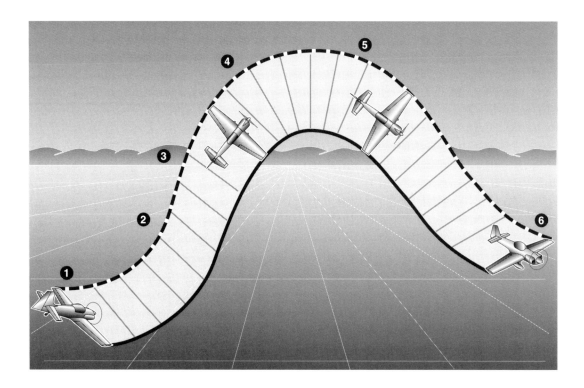

Piloting Technique

Following the normal HASELL check, find a line feature on the ground—a prominent road, railway line, runway or something that has a reasonable length in a straight line. Position the aircraft at 90° to this line, and use it as a guide. You don't have to be exact nor make corrections for wind, but it is nevertheless a very useful guide for alignment, orientation and position.

1. To enter the first wing-over, establish the aircraft in level flight with maximum continuous power, at around 3,000 feet AGL.

   As you approach at right angles to a line feature, clearly visible on the right, lower the nose, allow the aircraft to accelerate to V_{NO}, then gently pull up into a straight climb, until the nose is about 15° to 20° above the horizon.

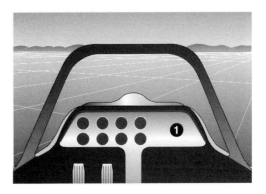

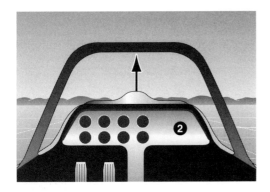

2. The plan is to enter a right-hand wing-over so that when you come down the other side, you are aligned with the line feature on the ground. Commence a positive pull up.

3. The next important thing is to visually scan—by looking ahead, then looking right, making sure it's clear, and then looking down to the line feature.

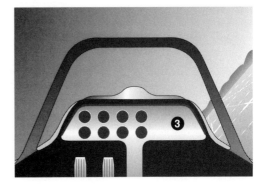

4. Roll to a bank angle of 90°, stop the roll, maintain the back pressure at 2*g* or so, and gently pull the nose around the horizon. Be ready to relax the back pressure slightly if the buffet begins. Of course, the nose will also be dropping through the horizon.

5. As the nose goes down and through the horizon, it should be approaching alignment with the line feature. Relax the back pressure, roll off the bank to wings-level and then apply gentle forward pressure to hold the nose in the entry attitude for the next maneuver as the aircraft accelerates back toward V_{NO}—aligned with the line feature.

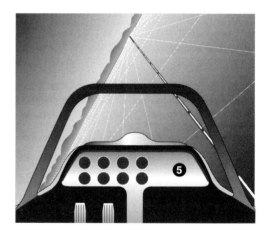

6. Obviously, you can raise the nose and go through the whole procedure again. It's a very valuable exercise to do alternate wing-overs, left and right, left and right, in a figure-eight pattern, using a line feature or features as a reference.

The wing-over through 180° is equally simple, provided the nose attitude is high before rolling on the bank and provided you *play* the back pressure sensitively through the pitching phase of the maneuver. It can be dangerous at low altitudes.

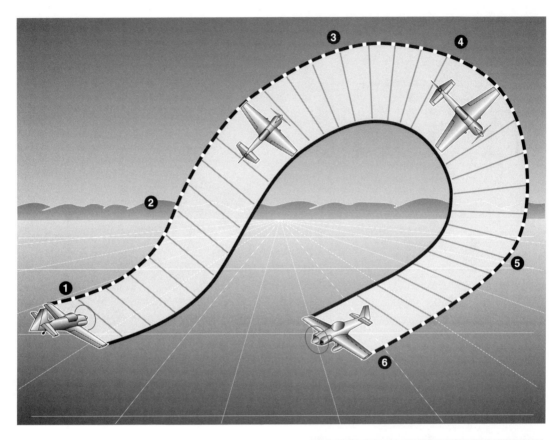

1. It is easy to lose too much energy in the first part of the maneuver and have to sacrifice altitude to regain airspeed in the second part—risky near the ground.

   Enter the maneuver in the same way as before, but judge how much additional airspeed (energy) you may need to complete the wing-over and be in a position to enter the next aerobatic maneuver.

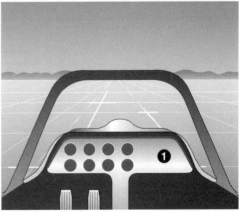

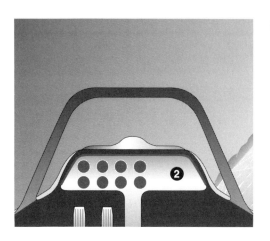

2. Raise the nose well above the horizon and maintain the back pressure as you roll.

3. Roll to 90° of bank or more and now *play* (adjust) the back pressure, buffet and bank angle so you will be rolling out in line with the feature with the nose below the horizon and the aircraft accelerating.

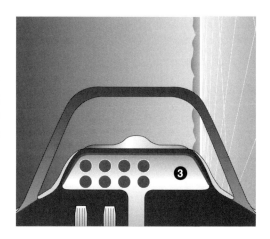

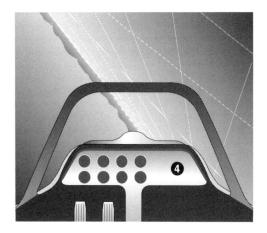

4. Allow the nose to fall through the horizon. Help it along if you need to by maintaining the back pressure and adjusting the bank angle.

5. Anticipate the roll-out and relax the back pressure and even apply some forward pressure to allow the aircraft to accelerate to the entry speed for the next maneuver.

6. Be precise with the alignment, attitude and airspeed when completing the wing-over.

These gentle wing-overs are performed with the power set at maximum continuous. As you become competent you may use full power and even idle to achieve the change of direction, attitudes and airspeed control you want from the maneuver. As was said, the wing-over can be anything you want it to be.

OK, let's be a little bit more adventurous. This time, run in at 90° to the line feature, as before, lower the nose, accelerate to V_{NO} and leave the pull up a little later than before. Pull up a little more firmly, say +3*g* and apply full power. Maintain the back pressure until the nose is about 30° above the horizon, look left, look down at the line feature, roll left to perhaps 120° or until the wings are at right angles to the line feature and pull the aircraft's nose around the corner, again maintaining about +3*g*. Hold the buffet. As the nose comes down through the horizon, anticipate alignment with line feature and roll the wings level. Apply slight forward pressure, accelerating downward until you have entry speed and entry attitude for the next maneuver which may be a barrel roll or a loop. Watch the propeller RPM as you accelerate.

Points of Airmanship

So much time has been spent describing what is a simple maneuver because it is the foundation for all maneuvering and for the development of feel, anticipation, coordination and judgment. It also is the means for developing a work cycle of looking out for other aircraft and looking in the direction you intend to be going.

The Chandelle

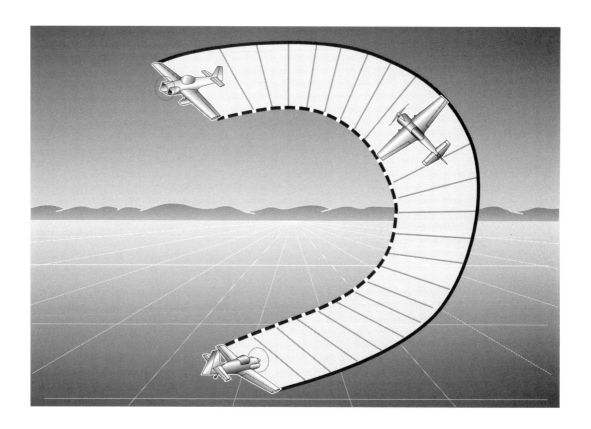

Description

The chandelle (candle) is identical to the first part of the wing-over but seeks to make maximum use of the change of airspeed to achieve the greatest altitude gain and change of direction. Thus, in its own way, it is a positioning and set-up maneuver for a subsequent entry. It is particularly good for positioning for a stall or spin entry. You decide the priority of direction, altitude or airspeed to complete the maneuver.

Aileron Roll

Description

The aileron roll differs from aircraft to aircraft, depending on the roll rate that can be achieved. In a high performance aircraft, the aileron roll is almost an instantaneous roll around the aircraft's longitudinal axis. Some aircraft can roll at more than 400°/second. Therefore, if the roll is begun at high airspeed, they can complete one or even several rolls before the momentum is lost and the flight path descends.

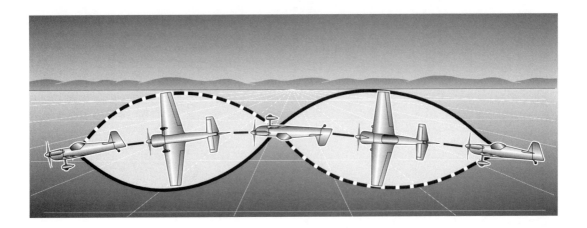

For a typical aerobatic training aircraft, the roll rate is more likely to be from 60 to 90° per second. Because of this reduced roll rate (and lower airspeed, momentum and thrust), it is essential to have the nose raised a reasonable distance above the horizon before you commence the roll so that the aircraft's flight path and momentum is upward through the first half of the roll and not too far downward, during the second half.

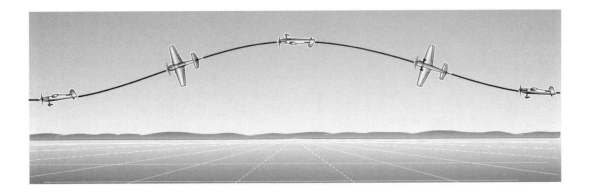

Piloting Technique

The easiest way to conduct the aileron roll is to enter in the same way as a wing-over. From maximum cruise, gently lower the nose, allow the aircraft to accelerate to about $2.5 \times V_S$, and then raise the nose symmetrically until the instrument glareshield is on the horizon (a normal climb attitude).

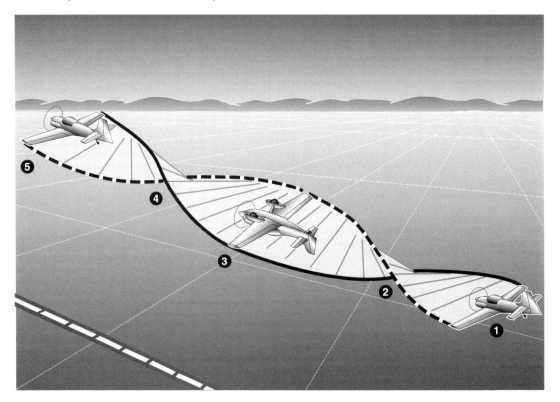

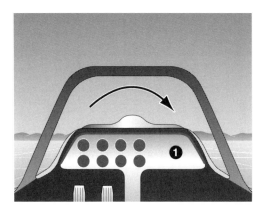

1. At this point, "check" the pitching motion, that is, stop the attitude momentarily and then smoothly apply full aileron deflection in the direction of roll (without applying forward or back pressure) and add a small amount of rudder in the direction of the roll—to balance any adverse aileron yaw.

2. At the wings-vertical position, maintain the aileron deflection but make sure to relax any back pressure.

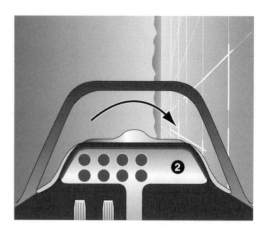

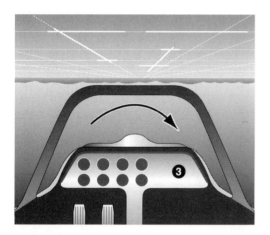

3. At the inverted position, relax any back pressure that may be there but don't push forward more than slightly. Maintain the roll rate. There is a tendency to relax the aileron pressure at this point and the aircraft staggers through the last half of the maneuver.

4. With 90° to go, again simply maintain the aileron with a little rudder to balance. Don't try to hold up the nose with top rudder (you'll learn about that in the slow roll).

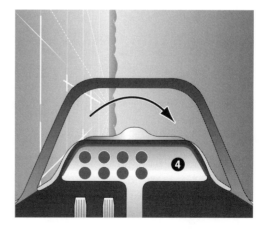

5. The nose will have dropped to the straight-and-level attitude or may be slightly lower, in which case you'll need to make an adjustment to the entry attitude for the next roll. Later, apply a little back pressure for the last 45° of the roll.

If the nose is a little low, it is of no matter. It is a useful guide to the entry attitude that should be used next time. Adjust it by the same amount.

At this stage of your training, don't worry about the nose falling through the maneuver or about forward pressure on the control column. Simply allow the aircraft to roll through 360° and center the controls as you come back to wings level.

Make the initial rolls opposite to the direction of engine rotation, so that the torque of the engine assists the roll. Later, you'll roll in the opposite direction and accept the reduced roll rate. U.S. horizontally-opposed engines rotate clock-wise when viewed from the cockpit so left-handed maneuvers are easier. U.K. in-line engines and some U.S. radial engines rotate the other way.

Points of Airmanship

Aileron application should always be smooth and full—never violent. Take about one-half second to reach full control deflection. Mind your knees, thighs and knee-pad (if you use one). If you are using full aileron warn your instructor or your passenger when you are about to commence the roll.

Loop

Description

The loop is very simply a straight pitch through 360° following a nominally circular flight path. There is positive, but not constant, g throughout.

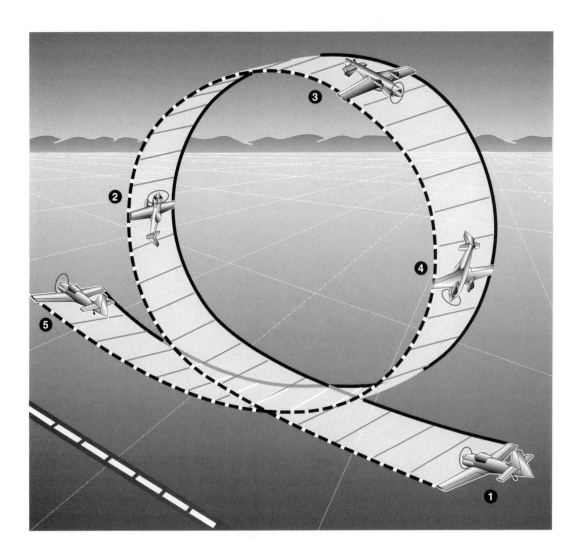

Piloting Technique

1. From now, commence all maneuvers from a 90° wing-over (to the left, if it's side-by-side seating and you are sitting on left side of the cockpit, to the right if you are in the right-hand seat). Plan the wing-over to arrive in line with your line feature in the attitude for entry to the loop. For most aircraft, this is with the canopy bow on the horizon accelerating toward the recommended entry speed for the loop.

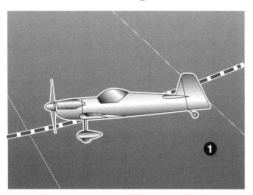
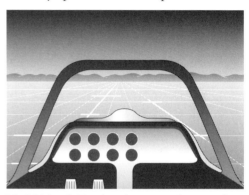

Entry speed will typically be 3 x V_S (or 85-90% of V_{NO})—but no slower than 2.5 × V_S. At 2 × V_S you can theoretically apply +4g which is sufficient for a loop, but remember you will be losing energy as soon as the g is applied.

You'll need to hold forward pressure in the dive to avoid the nose coming up. For aircraft with a fixed pitch propeller, monitor the engine RPM as the aircraft accelerates. When entry altitude and speed is reached, smoothly and positively apply back pressure, until you have +3.5 to 4g indicated and then hold that stick position. Apply full power. If the aircraft is installed with a yoke, make especially sure that you are pulling symmetrically—as the g can cause you to inadvertently apply aileron as well.

Ensure that the instrument glareshield is level as it passes through the horizon on the way up. As you approach the vertical, have a quick look to the left and right, to check the wings are equally displaced above the horizon.

2. The airspeed is reducing quite rapidly now. You'll need to increase right rudder pressure, because you still have relatively high power and low air speed—just like a normal climb. Don't look inside though.

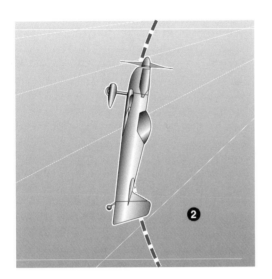

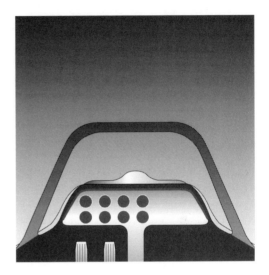

3. At this point, tilt your head right back until you can see the far horizon inverted through the canopy. Maintain the back pressure (the same stick position). There's a tendency to slacken at this stage. If you feel the buffet, slightly relax the back pressure.

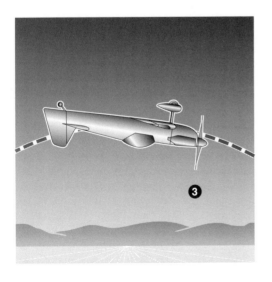

4. Be conscious of keeping the wings level over the top of the loop and keeping the right rudder applied. Allow the aircraft to come through the horizon inverted and to accelerate on the downward side. If you have relaxed the back pressure, through the top of the loop, reapply back pressure or return the control column back to where it was when you went into the loop. Remember: *Feel* your way.

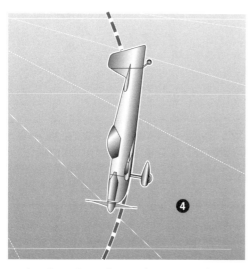

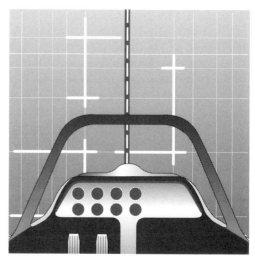

5. As the aircraft accelerates, reduce the right rudder. Pick up your line feature and adjust the bank, if necessary, to pull the nose of the aircraft along the line feature. Monitor the RPM and airspeed during the last 90° of the loop and control the speed with *g*. That is, be prepared to go to maybe +4.5*g* to keep the airspeed from increasing too quickly and to avoid excessive loss of altitude.

Like in a steep turn, there is no better feeling than flying through your own wash. Check the speed and altitude on completion of the maneuver and swap excess airspeed for altitude.

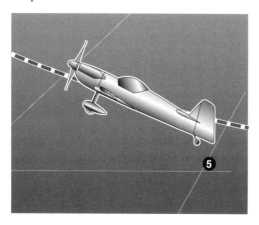

As the nose comes back through the horizon, continue to the climb attitude and complete a wing-over through 90° back to your entry conditions.

At this stage, relax in straight-and-level flight for a few moments, think about the maneuver, discuss it with your instructor and then start the exercise again. When you become more confident and proficient, you can string loops together with 180° wing-overs at either end or even do consecutive loops (the record is several hundred).

Don't forget the wing-over is not only the means of establishing the entry conditions for the maneuver. It's also your opportunity to have a good look around.

The common errors with the loop are:

- not having the wings exactly level as you pull up, thereby off-setting the axis of the loop;
- not applying rudder through the top half of the maneuver, allowing the aircraft to yaw/slip/slew slightly and, once again, skewing the loop to one side; and
- not applying the g positively enough at the beginning, or not applying sufficient g, in which case, the first third of the loop is very elongated and the aircraft doesn't have sufficient energy to fly through the top of the maneuver. It will fall over the top.

If your aircraft has a yoke instead of a stick then be careful to apply the back pressure symmetrically. Because your arm and hand are grasping one side of the yoke as the g forces take effect, there is a tendency for your arm to drop and inadvertently apply aileron. Therefore, the pull up will not be straight. This is a problem with any maneuvering with this type of control.

Is a Loop Round?

To fly an exactly circular path, and if the aircraft held a constant speed and pitch rate, the load factor would vary from say +4g at the bottom, +3g when vertical and +2g at the top.

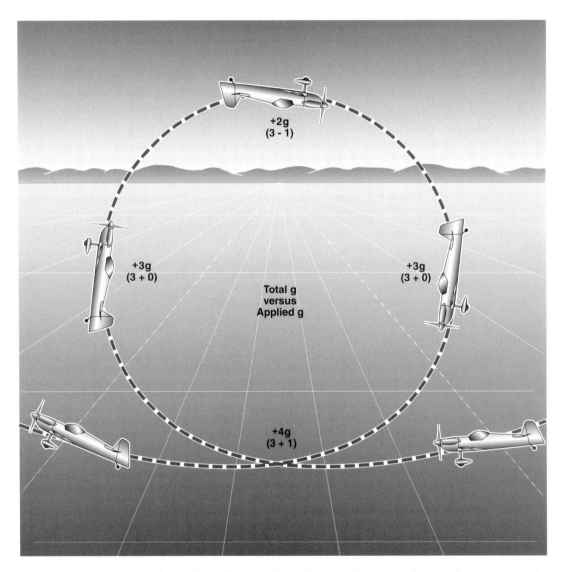

A circular path could also be followed if, as the speed varied, the pitch rate varied in proportion. This is basically what you are trying to do—without having any indicator in the cockpit. Load factor is a measure of speed and pitch rate so is a guide but you can't be flying around looking at the instruments as you continuously vary the pitch rate to adjust the load factor to correspond with the airspeed!

However, there is a practical solution. A nominally circular loop can be achieved by having a set entry speed and attitude, and applying a set load factor, say +4g. Then, by holding the stick position constant in that +4g position, the reducing airspeed will result in a reducing pitch rate and load factor which approximates the circular path. It only requires a minor adjustment if the buffet is encountered at the top.

At this point the pull force should be slightly relaxed and then reapplied as the aircraft begins to accelerate downhill. As the airspeed builds, a check that the load factor is also building back to +4g will result in a recovery close to the entry altitude. It's simple and it works.

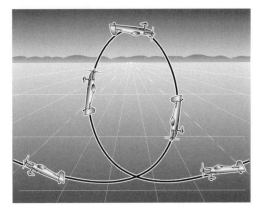

Uncompensated Loop

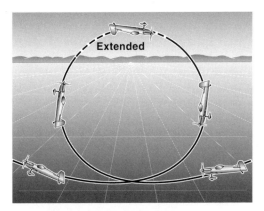

Extended Loop

For display flying, some pilots "play" the back pressure over the top of the loop by extending the inverted part to make up for the otherwise reduced distance traveled at this very low airspeed. They then have more room to position the aircraft on the down side of the loop. This changes the elongated shape to a circular one by extending the apex. Don't worry about these refinements at this stage. You are not flying in front of a crowd—not yet, anyway.

Points of Airmanship

Look ahead of the aircraft and well above the nose. Check the wingtips in the vertical position. Apply some rudder to balance the power at the reducing airspeed after you pass the vertical. Tilt your head back to find the far horizon, being sensitive to feel any onset of slight buffet. The application of g should be firm and positive, but not violent—about one second to reach +3.5g. Use the line feature on the down side and adjust the bank and rudder. Engine handling should be smooth and the RPM should be controlled.

Cuban Eights

Description

There are three forms of Cuban eight. The standard *Cuban eight* which is a loop to the 45° downward flight path followed by an aileron roll to erect flight, a pull up for a second loop to a 45° downward path and a second roll to erect flight with a straight dive recovery.

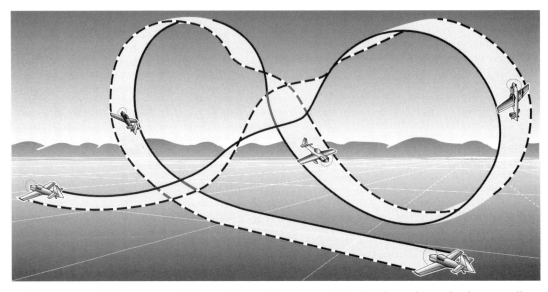

The *reverse Cuban* starts with straight pull up to a 45° climb path, and aileron roll to inverted. This is followed by a pull-through to a 45° climb, a further roll to inverted and a second pull-through to level flight.

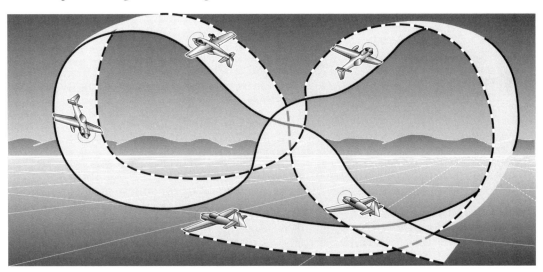

A *half cuban* is the loop to 45° down and a roll to erect flight, followed by a straight pull-out to level flight in the opposite direction.

The half Cuban could also be performed as the first half of the reverse Cuban.

Piloting Technique

All are simple maneuvers to perform as the aircraft is either accelerating during the downward roll or there is adequate airspeed from the pull up. The important point is to have a very clear reference line or feature on the horizon in both directions and to strive for a true 45° downward flight path. If the roll is too early and the nose attitude is too shallow, the aircraft will not accelerate for the second loop. If the nose is too steep, then there will be considerable loss of altitude and an excessive airspeed to begin the second loop.

The reverse Cuban has similar problems. If the pull up is shallow, then the aircraft will have too much energy when it heads downhill. If the pull up is too steep, there may not be sufficient energy to complete the roll. The essence of all Cubans is to start with the correct airspeed.

Airmanship

As with all aerobatic maneuvers, you need a clear horizon and a distinct line feature. Don't rush the maneuver. Fly the airplane, and let it stabilize at each point before changing the flight path, i.e. stop the pitch rate, pause and then roll; stop the roll then re-apply the back pressure. It is important to start with the correct entry speed. Keep looking where the aircraft *is going to be going,* not where it is, and not where it has been.

Barrel Roll

Description

The barrel roll is a combination of roll and pitch and yaw. The aircraft describes a horizontal spiral through the sky. Imagine a ribbon with the aircraft planform drawn on it at five points.

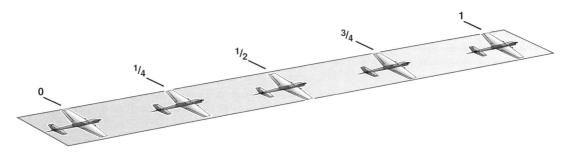

Then join one end of the ribbon to the other in the form of a ring or hoop, then if that stands vertical, we are describing the flight path of the aircraft through a loop. Note the aircraft is inverted half way through the maneuver but the pitch attitude is greatest at the 90° up and down points (one-quarter and three-quarters of the way through the maneuver, respectively).

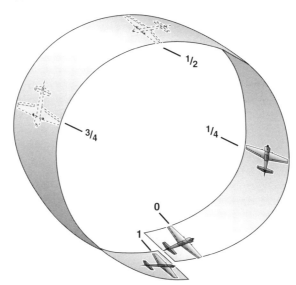

If you take the two ends of the ribbon, pull them straight, but twist the ribbon through 360° (it will resist the twist), you will see the planform of the aircraft as it goes through an aileron roll or a slow roll maneuver.

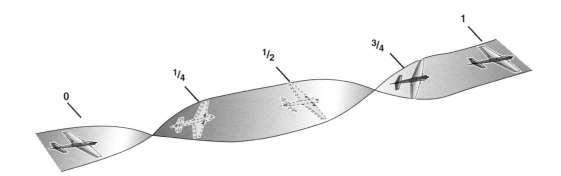

Note that it is inverted half way through the maneuver and if you started with a slightly climbing flight path the nose attitude is highest at the wings vertical point and lowest also at the three-quarter wings vertical point.

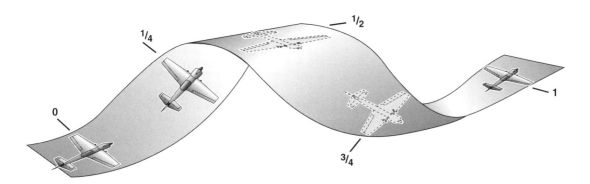

Now take the ribbon and displace the ends from the loop until they are half way between the straight hoop and the straight twist. You now have a maneuver that's somewhere between the loop and the aileron roll. You'll see the ribbon describes the horizontal spiral previously discussed. This is the barrel roll. Note that the inverted position is at the highest point of the roll and that the steepest nose-up and nose-down attitudes are at the wings-vertical positions.

Particularly note that the top of the barrel roll is when the aircraft is inverted. It has to be. The only way an aircraft (other than the AV-8 which has vectored thrust) can generate centripetal force toward the center of the roll (which it must have to change the flight path in that direction) is to use part of the lift force of the wings. The lift generates the centripetal force. You'll find some publications which show the aircraft with the wings vertical at the top of the barrel roll. The argument has gone on since the maneuver was invented. But it is a very important error. Misunderstanding the apogee of the roll has contributed to several fatal accidents.

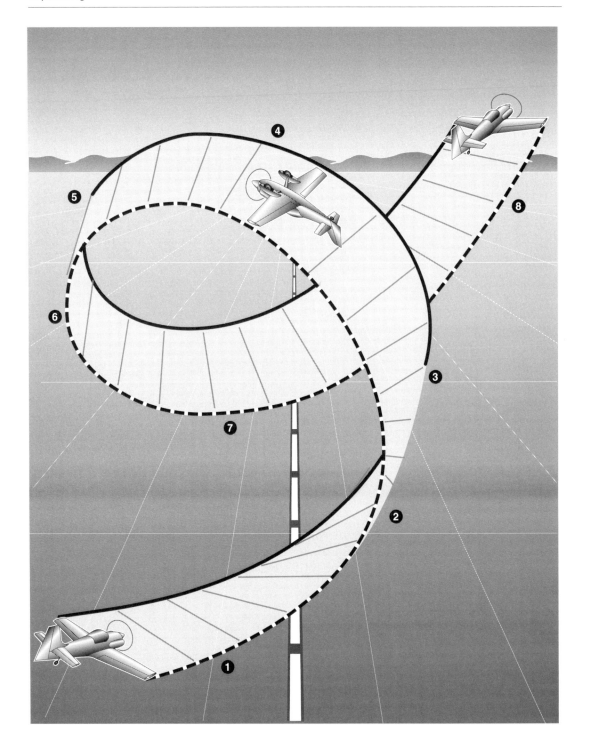

Note also that the pitch attitude is steepest at the wings vertical point and lowest at the three-quarter roll wings vertical position. This has been the cause of confusion with the barrel roll. *The attitude is steepest at the wings vertical point but the flight path is still climbing until it reaches the inverted position.* Any attempt to pull the nose down after the wings vertical point will cause the second half of the roll to bottom out.

If you reach the wings-level, inverted position, with the nose passing through the horizon, there is no way you can complete the roll without "barrelling-out" of the bottom. It is the greatest cause of problems with the barrel roll and it's also been the cause of many fatal display accidents. Once the nose is committed low and you have a limited roll-rate, then you are a goner.

The wings must be generating lift toward the center of the roll at all times for the aircraft to change its flight path in that direction and the aircraft must climb through the first half of the roll to be able to recover at the entry altitude in the remaining half.

Piloting Technique

To enter the barrel roll, start with the usual wing-over through 90°. Set the aircraft up 500 feet or so above the entry altitude, at 90° to the line feature, and you'll find it works out more comfortably if you do a left wing-over into a right hand barrel roll or a right hand wing-over into a left hand barrel roll.

There are two ways to select and use a reference for the roll
- pick a point 60–90° off the nose in the direction of the roll. This will be the reference for alignment at the inverted position;

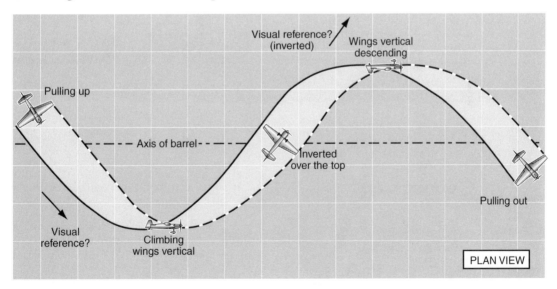

- or pick your normal line feature and exit the wing-over 30°–45° through the axis, planning to be the corresponding angle off-axis in the other direction, as you go over the top.

- The latter is an easier method if you have been used to using a line feature.

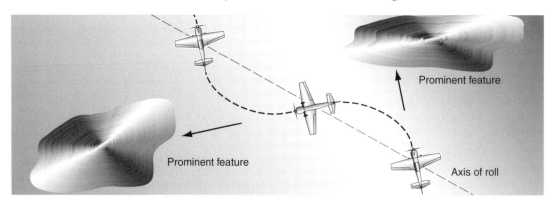

Prominent feature

Prominent feature

Axis of roll

(Refer to the diagram on page 112 for an overview of this maneuver.)

1. Because the engine torque in most aircraft favors the left roll, plan a right wing-over into a left roll. Raise the nose into the wing-over, look right, roll right, pull the aircraft around the corner and pull through the line feature by about 30°. By this time, the nose would have dropped through the horizon. Continue to pull and roll until you have the canopy bow on the horizon. Stop the roll and allow the aircraft to accelerate to the entry speed. Smoothly apply $+2g$ to $+3g$ and continue the nose through the horizon until the instrument glareshield passes through the horizon.

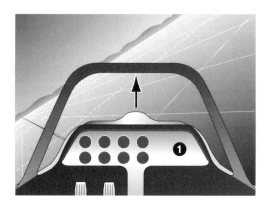

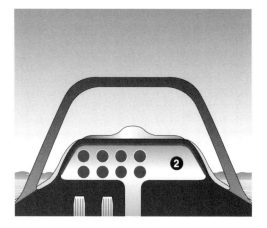

2. At this point, introduce about half aileron deflection. You'll need a little rudder to balance—in the same direction as the applied aileron—but unlike other rolls, *maintain the back pressure.* This is the most important stage of the barrel roll.

3. One could say that the first part is roll and pull, the second part is more roll but less pull, and the last part, increasing pull and less roll.

Allow the aircraft then to zoom (due to its momentum), maintain the roll and pitch rates until the aircraft approaches the wings-vertical position.

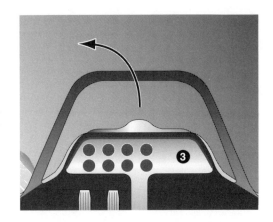

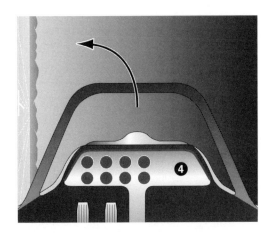

4. At this point the nose should be well and truly above the horizon. With the reducing airspeed, the roll rate will tend to reduce, so for the second quarter of the roll, you'll need to increase the aileron deflection and at the same time relax the back pressure a little.

5. The inverted top-of-the-roll position, should be equivalent to the inverted top-of-the-loop position, that is, with the canopy bow on the horizon and the instrument glareshield still well above the horizon.

At this reduced airspeed, you'll need slightly more rudder to balance and a little more aileron to keep the roll-rate constant.

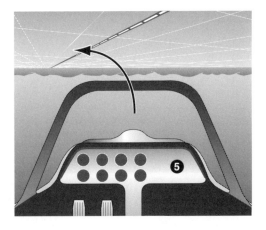

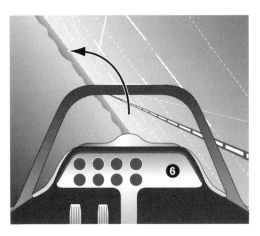

6. The aircraft will now start to accelerate on the downward half of the roll, you'll need to reintroduce additional back pressure (yes, back pressure) and slightly reduce the amount of aileron deflection to continue a constant roll rate through the bottom of the maneuver.

7. The increasing back pressure and reducing aileron is the second most important part of a successful barrel roll. It takes some finesse to balance the increase of one with the decrease of the other.

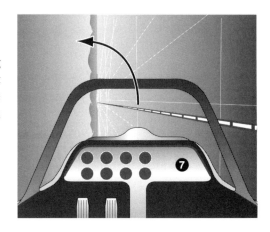

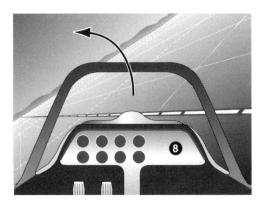

8. As the aircraft accelerates, you can use reduced rudder deflection to balance. The aircraft will roll nicely out on the line feature, pointing 30° or so off-axis—the same way as you did on entry. Your aircraft may have an offset vertical stabilizer or an offset engine to partly counter the torque and slipstream effects. Think about this when planning the maneuver.

The barrel roll is a very comfortable and pleasant maneuver but difficult to fly accurately and in balance—and therefore is a very good maneuver to practice. Ultimately, you'll be able to rest your knee-pad or other soft object on the instrument glareshield and leave it there for the duration of the roll, just as Bob Hoover does with his cup of water.

Common errors with the barrel roll are:

- not getting the nose high enough at the beginning, before introducing the aileron;
- allowing the roll rate to reduce over the top and therefore allowing the nose to become too low at the commencement of the second half of the roll; or
- going from the 90° wings-vertical position to the inverted position while maintaining too much back pressure—thereby pulling the nose across and down and giving an insufficiently high nose attitude to commence the second half of the roll.

The barrel roll can be done with a variety of roll versus pitch ratios. It can be loop-like with very high pitch angles or roll-like with small pitch angles. A typical barrel roll contains 360° of roll and about 40° of pitch (10° nose down to 20° nose up to 10° nose down again— a total of 40° traversed). Thus the roll/pitch ratio and rates are nearly ten to one. Start on the easy side by raising the nose to a good 20° or 30° above the horizon and rolling fast rather than slowly. Adjust the ratio of roll to pitch during the last quarter of the maneuver.

The combination of aileron and elevator can stretch the "barrel" from a very large elongated roll not far displaced from the loop, down to a very tight rapid barrel roll, not unlike a curved aileron roll. For most purposes, somewhere in between is a good balance. The 30°–45° off-set from the line feature is a good reference.

Having completed the barrel roll to the left, continue the nose up through the horizon, into a left-hand wing-over, back to the 90° position.

Eventually you'll go from that left wing-over, into a right-hand barrel roll, into a right wing-over, into a left-hand barrel roll, into a left wing-over and so on. It makes a very nice, flowing sequence. You can, of course, put a loop in the middle there. We'll look at a sequence in the next chapter.

Points of Airmanship

Look out while flying the maneuver. You need a clearly defined horizon. Feel the back pressure and observe the roll rate. If you do not feel good about the way the maneuver is progressing, remove all back pressure and roll to wings-level.

Hammerhead

Description

In very simple terms, the hammerhead, or stall turn, is a pull up to a vertical zoom, and before all forward momentum is lost, the aircraft is yawed through 180° into a vertically downward dive. After accelerating to normal flying speed, the aircraft is recovered to level flight. In the process, the aircraft has obviously reversed direction.

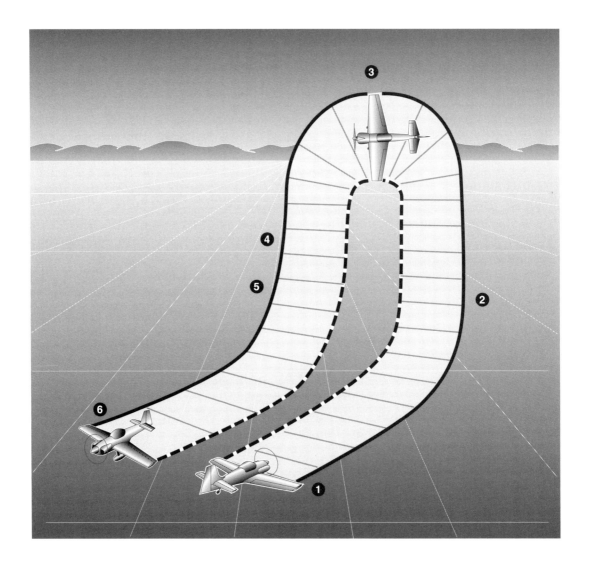

There are various combinations and permutations which add various types of roll to the upward and downward segments of the hammerhead but we'll stay with the basic maneuver. It is a fairly simple maneuver and is comfortable to perform. There is little stress on the aircraft or pilot other than in the pull up and the dive recovery. However, there is a slight feeling of insecurity (a "pregnant" pause) at the vertical, no airspeed stage but you will soon get used to this if you perform the maneuver regularly.

Vertical Attitude

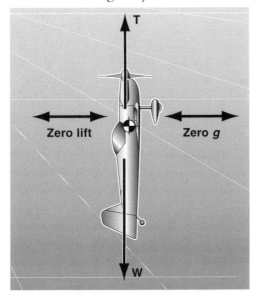
Forces when Vertical

The hammerhead is a maneuver where the aircraft is pitched to a vertical path and held at $0g$ until well below V_S. The airflow from the propeller allows some control power for the elevators and more particularly the rudder, and this is used to yaw the aircraft through 180° until it is facing vertically down. Then the aircraft has to be allowed to accelerate in $0g$ flight until it has sufficient airspeed to apply $+3g$ or so for the dive recovery (later you may use a negative g recovery in a competition aircraft). So the hammerhead isn't a stall, at all, at all—after all.

Consider for a moment, the aircraft at the top of the zoom at very low airspeed with full power. Full rudder is applied with engine torque assisting or countering the yaw, depending on the direction of the yaw.

All aircraft with U.S. horizontally-opposed engines will hammerhead left far more easily than right because the engine torque is assisting. Interestingly, there is a rolling moment due to the induced effect of the yaw—which must be countered with gross use of opposite aileron (very low airspeed over the surfaces).

Note: you now have full pro-spin controls—but of course, we are nowhere near the stalling angle-of-attack.

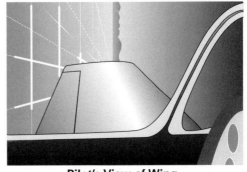
Pilot's View of Wing

The gyroscopic precession of the engine/propeller combination will cause a nose-up pitching moment as the aircraft yaws left (left yaw causes pitch up with a clockwise direction of engine rotation—as viewed from the cockpit). Therefore, slight forward control pressure is required to maintain the yawing plane.

The hammerhead is a difficult yet unique maneuver to experience as the airspeed is close to zero and the aircraft behavior is dominated by the slipstream, torque and prop-wash effects.

Piloting Technique

The hammerhead is identical to the loop for the first 90° of pitch. Same entry, same look-out, same wing-over, same straight pull up, same full power, checking that the glareshield is parallel to the horizon as it passes through.

1. A straight pull up is critical for the hammerhead. Maintain the g until you reach the vertical position with reference to the wing tips. Go slightly beyond the vertical to allow for angle-of-incidence. It is better to err on the overly steep side. You will need to apply progressive right rudder to counter the yaw as the aircraft decelerates.

With practice, you will have a second to check each wingtip is the same distance above the horizon—and therefore the vertical path is straight.

2. At the vertical position, simply "check" the pitching motion and hold the aircraft in a climbing flight path with forward pressure. Now look left (for a left-hand hammerhead).

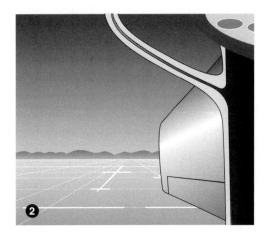

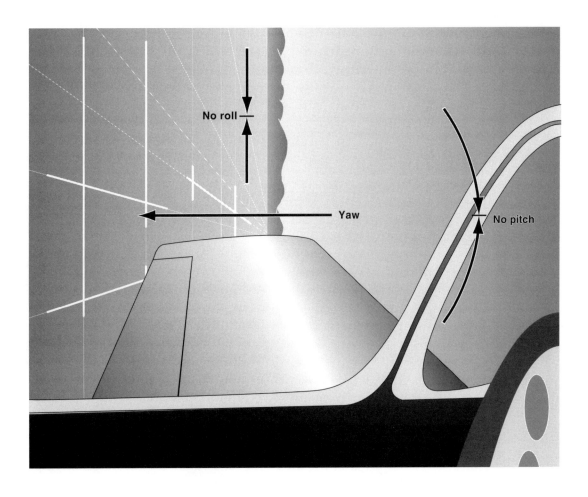

3. After a momentary pause, firmly and progressively apply full left rudder. With the left rudder, there will initially be slight reluctance and then the aircraft will start to yaw left. As it does so, the secondary effect of yaw causes the aircraft to tend to roll in the same direction. Thus you'll need left rudder, forward pressure to hold zero *g* and some right aileron to keep the plane of the yaw flat in relation to the vertical axis of the aircraft—and the vertical axis of the aircraft horizontal to the earth. Look at the nose.

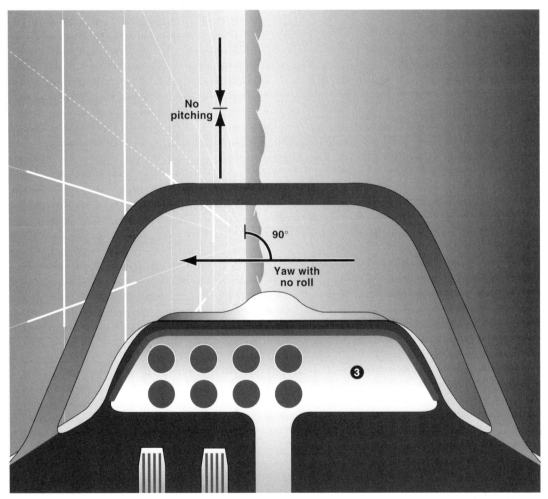

As the nose slices through the horizon, check for vertical alignment and, if necessary, make an aileron input to correct. You may reduce the engine power at this stage but it is not essential. Some aircraft need to have the power reduced for a right-hand hammerhead but not necessarily for the left. As the aircraft points down, it will want to oscillate like a pendulum as it goes through the nose-down vertical position and until the airspeed builds. You may use the rudder actively to stop this oscillation.

4. You can apply fairly coarse right rudder and then left rudder to check this oscillation. Of course, at this very low airspeed, there is not a great deal of control power.

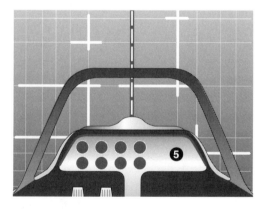

5. As the aircraft accelerates, check your reference line and smoothly and firmly apply the same amount of back pressure as you would for recovery from the last half of the loop.

In a right-hand hammerhead you may need to reduce the engine power as soon as the yaw rate is established. Otherwise the engine effects will resist the yaw.

A hammerhead to the right is a little more difficult, because you have the engine resisting you over the top. Same entry on pull up, look to the right 90° check, introduce some right rudder, while you still have the slipstream effect of the engine, and as soon as the aircraft starts to yaw, slowly and smoothly reduce the power. The aircraft will then slice through the horizon, into the nose-down position and accelerate. Be careful not to exceed the engine RPM when reintroducing the power.

6. Level attitude—convert excess airspeed to altitude. Monitor RPM and adjust power if necessary.

The hammerhead is pleasant, but less controlled maneuver than previous ones, because for a moment at the top of the maneuver, the aircraft is almost stationary, with high power, reduced control power except for the rudder and elevator in the propwash, and no airflow over the ailerons. Thus, you are relying on momentum and then gravity for the aircraft to come out in the right direction.

There is a tendency not to be truly vertical. Being less than vertical, or past vertical, makes it more difficult to yaw with reference to the vertical plane. There is also a tendency, if there is any reverse airflow as the aircraft starts to slide backward for it to pitch rather than yaw. Then it becomes a tailslide, with the nose pitching violently down or over the top.

Points of Airmanship

You really need a clearly-defined horizon for the hammerhead. The aircraft is in a regime where it could easily depart from controlled flight (large rudder deflections, potentially large aileron deflections, very low airspeed, high power and the aircraft starting to slide backward). If the aircraft starts to auto-rotate or to tailslide, you must close the throttle, center the controls and wait. It can be quite a violent reversal and change of direction. Simply hang on until the aircraft is accelerating downward and you have normal aerodynamic control restored. If you are worried about tail-sliding then apply rudder but be ready to prevent it from going to full deflection and being damaged.

Inverted Flight

Description

Inverted flight is simply flying straight-and-level and balanced—upside down. However, you must consider that the wing may have a positive angle-of-incidence and positive camber.

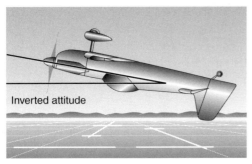

Inverted Attitude

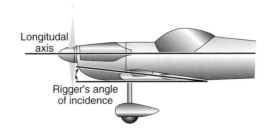

Erect Attitude

The attitude for inverted flight will be markedly nose high (above the horizon) probably equivalent to the climb attitude reversed—that is, canopy bow on the horizon, inverted.

Pilot's View when Inverted

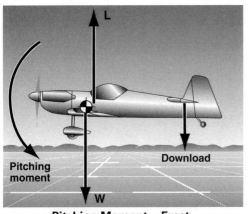

Pitching Moment—Erect

In erect flight, the aircraft is balanced in pitch, and the horizontal stabilizer is rigged so that it has a down-load. This counters the nose-down pitching moment.

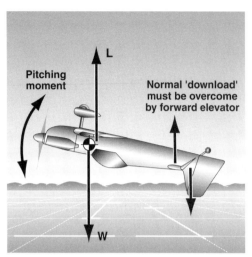

Pitching Moment—Inverted

When the aircraft is inverted, this has the result of trying to lower the nose relative to the horizon. Even more forward stick is required, especially at low airspeeds. There may not be enough control power to maintain level inverted flight at airspeeds slower than normal cruise speed. When inverted, the stalling speed is also increased—as the camber of the airfoil is contrary to the curvature of the airflow.

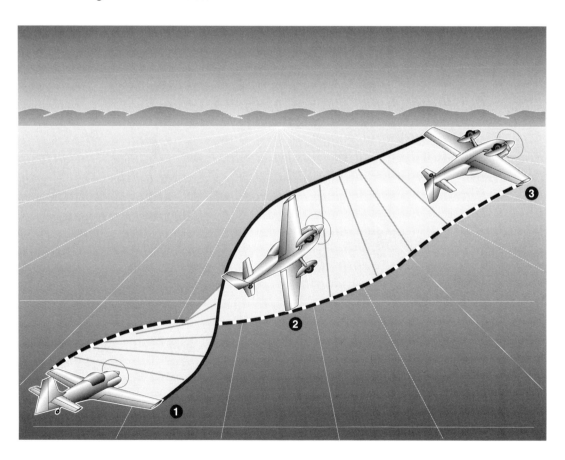

Piloting Technique

Rolling to Inverted Flight

1. From a wing-over, accelerate to fast cruise speed, say twice V_S, raise the nose to the climb attitude or slightly higher, "check" the pitch rate and apply full aileron with a little rudder to balance.

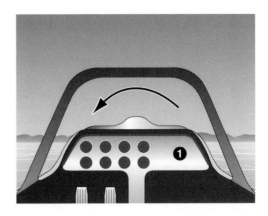

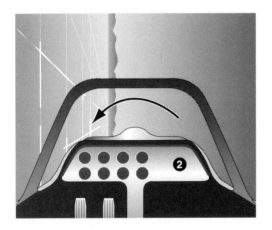

2. Apply some top rudder as the wings pass the vertical, and ensure that the positive g is relaxed as the roll is started and then, after wings-vertical, progressively apply forward pressure until inverted.

3. Maintain the aileron deflection as you push forward. There is a tendency to neutralize it. Typically, the inverted flight attitude is with the canopy bow on the horizon. It may take almost full forward stick to maintain inverted flight if the aircraft has a cambered airfoil and a positive angle-of-incidence. At this point, all of the dust, dirt and loose particles from the cockpit floor will fall past your eyes. (Yes, it happens). Loose shoulder straps will float in front of your face and the headset lead may snake across your field–of–view.

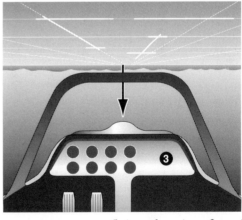

The *floaters* can be disconcerting but try to concentrate on flying the aircraft and maintain the straight, level and balanced inverted attitude. **Note**: the rudder is *not* reversed in inverted flight. All of the controls always work in the same sense—*as viewed by the pilot.* Always *step on the ball* (if you have an inverted balance ball).

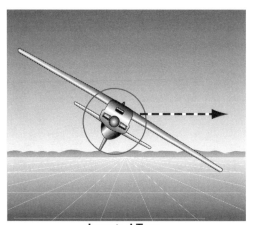

Inverted Turn

Also, when inverted, adverse aileron yaw operates in the same sense—*as viewed by the pilot.* If you wanted to enter an inverted turn from inverted flight with an aileron input say to the left (for a left turn as perceived from the ground), then the adverse yaw (to the right as perceived by the pilot) is in fact, not adverse to the turn! (It makes a good debate over a beer.)

To stay level inverted, maintain the pitch attitude by normal pushing and pulling on the control column.

Similarly, keep the wings level to the horizon as you would normally. Use the rudder to balance by looking into the distance and keeping straight. The balance ball is one reference that does not work inverted although aircraft capable of sustained inverted flight will have an inverted balance ball for this purpose.

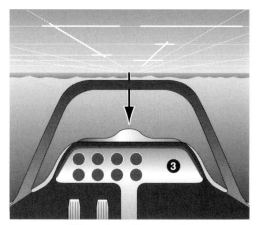

Wings Level Inverted

Rolling to Erect Flight

Return to erect flight by completing a slow roll or aileron roll. Apply rudder in the same direction as the aileron. This will overcome adverse aileron yaw and help to keep the nose up through the wings-vertical position. Bring the control column back through neutral so that back pressure is applied for the last 90°.

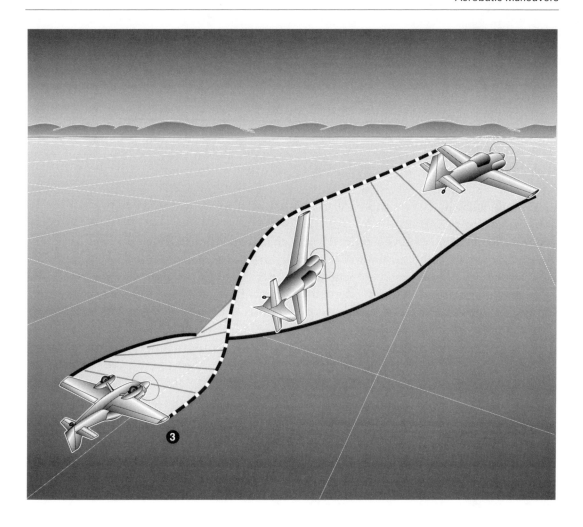

Points of Airmanship

Double-check that your harness and that of your passenger is *completely* tight and secure. Double-check there are no loose objects. Do not enter the roll below the recommended speed. If the aircraft is too slow, the extra amount of forward pressure required to maintain inverted level flight, and the fact that stall speed inverted is likely to be higher than in erect flight, may be sufficient to stall the wing inverted and thus create the possibility of an inverted departure and spin entry. Similarly, a violent application of forward stick approaching the inverted position may cause the same result or even an outside snap roll.

Check and observe any limitations that apply to your aircraft as far as inverted flight and engine handling is concerned. If the engine coughs, relax the forward pressure immediately and roll to wings level, closing the throttle at the same time.

Slow Roll

Description

The slow roll is known as a coordination exercise but in fact, the control inputs are contrary to almost any other maneuver. They are coordinated and yet the aircraft is totally out of balance. The slow roll used to be deliberately slow as the longer the duration of the roll, the more difficult the coordination and the maintenance of a constant roll rate. Also it used to take a long time to fly the full length of the field over which the roll was being performed. Nowadays, the slow roll is only called *slow* because it is slower than the aileron roll (which in most aircraft with limited roll rate, is done with full aileron deflection). For the slow roll, about half aileron deflection is used. Slow does not refer to low airspeed.

More significant than the time taken is that the slow roll follows a nominally level flight path whereas the aileron roll is simply a roll using aileron alone and the flight path during the roll is not corrected to any great extent—in fact, as we know, it changes from a slightly ascending to a slightly descending path. Further, no negative g is experienced in the inverted attitude of the aileron roll whereas the slow roll passes through the true inverted flight attitude and $-1g$.

In the slow roll, the flight path is managed throughout to maintain straight-and-level through the knife-edge and inverted stages of the roll. Thus the aircraft changes from positive to negative angles-of-attack and from balanced flight to high sideslip angles in each direction—while at the same time, maintaining a nominally constant rate-of-roll.

A perfect roll would look like this.

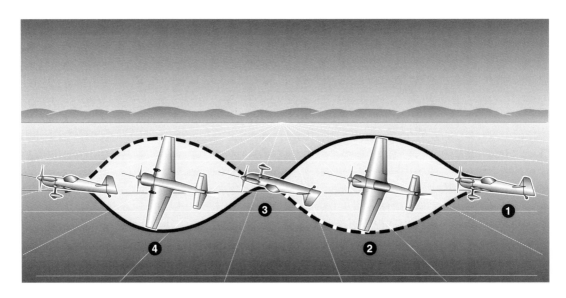

However, most aircraft require a slightly raised nose attitude on entry to achieve a level attitude on completion.

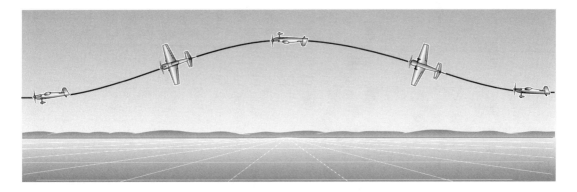

Piloting Technique

Before commencing the slow roll, which some would say is a difficult, uncomfortable and unbalanced maneuver, you'll first explore inverted flight and practice the first half of the roll to the inverted attitude.

The aircraft you fly, may be restricted to 30 seconds of inverted flight, due to falling oil pressure. It may be restricted to even less by the lack of an inverted fuel system. Alternatively, it may allow unlimited inverted flight. If it is restricted, you may roll to inverted, hold it momentarily, recognize the attitude and the control positions and then return to erect level flight. To return from inverted to level flight is more difficult than the first half. As the aircraft is rolled, the forward pressure is progressively relaxed until there is none as the aircraft passes the wings vertical position. Then there is a need for back pressure and some top rudder as the aircraft rolls through 45° and then reducing rudder as the aircraft reaches level.

1. Next, you'll attempt the complete slow roll. To enter, start with a normal wing-over entry, pulling the nose up until the instrument glareshield is at least on the horizon and check (stop the pitching).

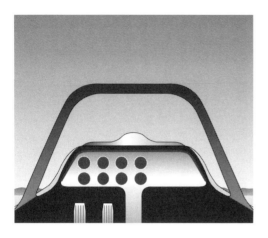

In lower performance aircraft, the nose may have to be as high as 20°–30° above the horizon. Smoothly apply half aileron in the direction of roll, and on this occasion, start to introduce opposite, yes, opposite rudder (adverse aileron yaw helps us here).

2. So left aileron, rolling left and because you want to roll around the point, apply right rudder to stop the nose moving to the left and ease the control column forward.

As the wings approach the vertical position, you'll have almost full right rudder (top rudder) applied to stop the nose dropping, and any back pressure you had will now be neutralized.

As you go through the wings vertical attitude, you'll need to apply progressive forward pressure to hold the nose up.

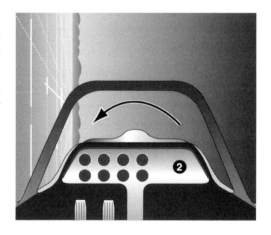

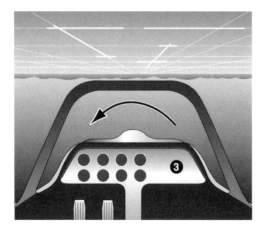

3. As the roll continues, rudder is progressively reduced so that it is centered at the inverted attitude.

As the aircraft approaches the inverted attitude there is a tendency to apply insufficient forward pressure. There is also a tendency to reduce the aileron deflection and so the roll rate deteriorates while the nose continues to drop.

4. After the inverted position the roll rate is maintained and progressive (large) left rudder is introduced. This last half is the difficult part as the aileron has to be maintained, more rudder introduced, and then reduced after wings vertical, and the stick has to move through the trimmed position to progressive back pressure for the last quarter of the roll. It is likely that the airspeed will have decayed during the roll and so more back pressure is required than you would expect to keep the nose up.

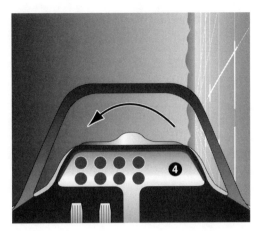

Using a Visual Reference

If there is a cloud you can use as a reference, simply use rudder and stick as required, to keep the nose in one position as you roll through 360°. (Sounds easy!)

Points of Airmanship

Even though the inverted position is transitory, you will experience all of the effects of negative g ($-1g$). The same considerations apply. If the engine fails or hesitates, or the oil pressure warning illuminates, relax the back pressure and complete the roll. Close the throttle as you do so. If it "falls" out, that is, the nose attitude cannot be maintained when inverted, again relax the forward pressure and roll while closing the throttle. If you are pushing firmly on the control column and you experience any airframe or control buffet, relax at least some of the forward pressure, and accept the altitude loss as you complete the roll. Chances are that the entry speed was too low, or you started the roll a little too soon.

Immelmann Turn

Description

The Immelmann (roll–off–the–top) was developed by a World War I pilot named Max Immelmann as a rapid way of reversing direction without loss of altitude, in the least space, and with minimal loss of energy. Like the gentler chandelle, kinetic energy (air-speed) is exchanged for potential energy (altitude). The Immelmann consists of a loop to inverted flight and an aileron roll or slow roll (or even a snap roll) to level flight. Thus the aircraft changes direction quickly.

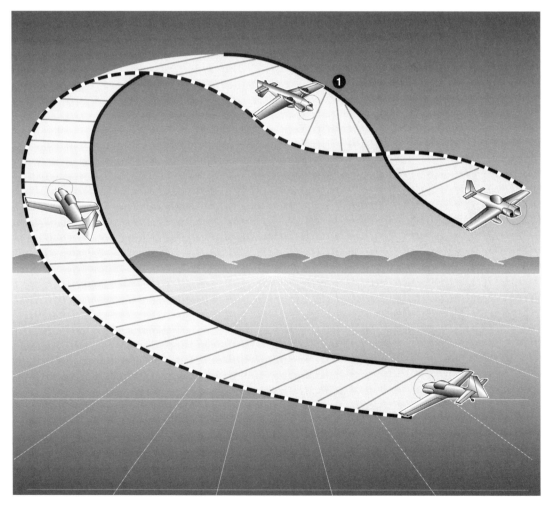

The Immelmann is the same as a half Cuban eight, except that the roll is completed at the apex in order to maximize altitude gain.

1. The term *slow* roll is not strictly correct, as there is no intention to roll slowly but the term is used to describe the fact that in this case, the pilot holds negative *g* briefly while the pitch rate is *checked*—rather than allowing the nose to drop during the roll. Aircraft with a decent roll rate will simply roll out while those with a low rate-of-roll at this low speed will have to be held level during the roll.

For aircraft with limited inverted flight capability, it is far more logical and comfortable to allow the nose to fall through the roll and to roll with aileron, coordinated with rudder.

Piloting Technique

The true Immelmann is not an easy maneuver. Entry speed and load factors are higher than a loop so that the aircraft has more energy to roll at the top. The aircraft is slow at the start of the roll and almost full forward stick is required to maintain inverted level flight. Full aileron deflection is needed (with possible pronounced adverse yaw), the engine is at high power and as the aircraft rolls, there will be considerable sideslip. This is a regime where an inverted stall and departure from controlled flight (and an inverted spin) is possible unless the aircraft has plenty of energy and control power.

Some aircraft will enter an inverted spin from here. Talk this through with your instructor. Some references describe an alternative Immelmann with a half-barrel roll. This is illogical as it will result in completing the maneuver off-line—the axis of a barrel roll being offset from the aircraft direction of flight. However, it can be completed quite pleasantly with a half snap roll.

Points of Airmanship

During the pull up, the aircraft is at high speed and high *g*. Control inputs should be tempered. The roll needs to be started with the nose well above the horizon, and care is needed.

Split-S

Description

The split-s is simply that—a half roll to inverted followed by the second half of a loop. The roll can be an aileron roll or a slow roll but it is vital to start the half loop at low airspeed and with a high inverted nose attitude.

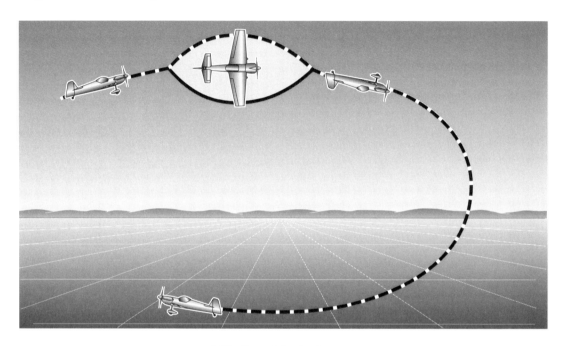

Piloting Technique

The easiest method for the aircraft and the pilot, is to pull up slightly from below cruise speed to the normal climb attitude, pause, roll to inverted, pause and smoothly apply positive g—being careful to avoid the buffet. Once the g is applied, the airspeed will be contained and as the aircraft accelerates, a normal loop is completed. The throttle can be retarded, or, if necessary, closed once the aircraft is accelerating downhill.

Points of Airmanship

This is a risky maneuver if entered with a nose-low attitude. Make a distinct pull up before the roll. Any excess speed or acceleration in the first quarter of the maneuver is dangerous—if in doubt, close the throttle, roll upright and pull out. Conversely, a slow entry or excessive buffet at the beginning can delay acceleration to maneuvering speed and can actually cause the aircraft to lose more altitude in the maneuver. It can stagger rather than fly through the maneuver. It is a matter of playing back pressure against increasing airspeed.

Knife-Edge Flight

Description

Unless the aircraft has upward momentum, any maneuver requiring 90° of bank will result in a loss of altitude. Whether in sustained straight flight at 90° of bank, or partially through a slow roll or a hesitation roll, there is a need to generate lift from sources other than the wings—otherwise the flight path will curve downward. High performance aircraft with high roll rates can momentarily raise the nose (upward path), roll rapidly and complete the roll before the flight path descends below horizontal. For a true horizontal path though, we have to use other means to sustain the level path.

Vertical wings can contribute nothing to maintaining a level flight path. Gravity can only be balanced by a side force from the fuselage, vertical stabilizer and rudder (with a contribution from the thrust vector). This requires that the aircraft has sufficient rudder power to hold the nose up (in relation to the horizon) against the directional stability of the aircraft which tries to cancel any sideslip. If the rudder power is sufficient to do this, then the aircraft can be made to maintain a high sideslip angle, and the side force from the fuselage and vertical stabilizer then generates the "lift" to balance the force of gravity.

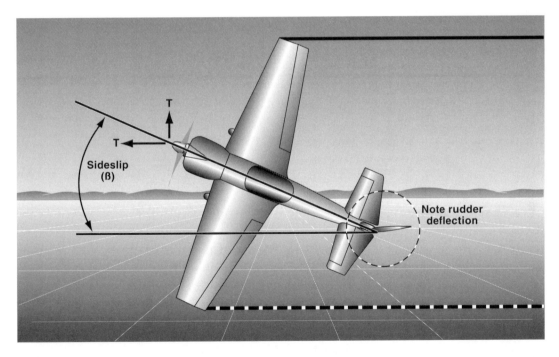

The engine also contributes a little. The thrust from the propeller at this high sideslip angle has a component at 90° to the flight path, as well as the major component along the flight path.

Some aircraft can sustain this sideslip just enough to complete a rolling maneuver. Others, such as the Pitts Special, can fly indefinitely this way.

At such high sideslip angles, there is a dihedral effect too. The lower wing presents greater frontal area to the relative airflow and unless there is exactly zero lift, there may be a small rolling moment toward erect flight. If the wing has a positive angle-of-incidence or camber, then the effect is more pronounced.

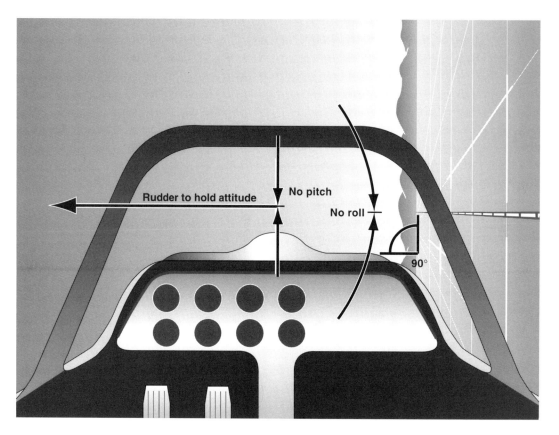

Piloting Technique

Before entering the roll the aircraft needs a nose-high entry attitude corresponding to the attitude needed at the 90° wings-vertical position. Then the roll should be done quickly to the wings-vertical position. A large amount of rudder will be required to keep the nose at the equivalent attitude to the entry position.

Points of Airmanship

For most aircraft, a reasonable entry airspeed is required so that the side force is sufficient to maintain level flight. At lower airspeeds, full rudder may be insufficient to hold the nose up and may even stall. Full rudder should only be applied at speeds below V_A.

Hesitation Rolls

Description

The hesitation roll consists of 4, 8 or even 16 hesitations (pauses) during the roll. To be completed in a reasonable space with reasonable airspeed and with distinct pauses, it requires quite harsh control inputs. It's a "bang-bang," full aileron/no aileron type of maneuver and not particularly pleasant—especially for a passenger.

It is much easier in a higher performance aircraft with high momentum and high rates-of-roll. Adverse aileron yaw is also a problem at lower airspeeds.

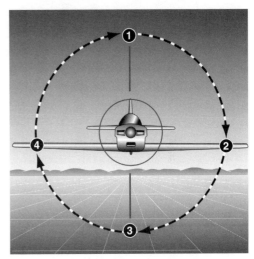

Four-Point Hesitation Roll

Piloting Technique

Let's restrain ourselves to a four-point roll. Entry is the same as a slow roll but full aileron is used and a higher entry speed. (At airspeeds above V_A, which may be necessary for some aircraft, initially use less than full control deflection.) As the aircraft approaches the wings-vertical position, the roll is checked and the nose held momentarily with top rudder. The aileron is suddenly reapplied and the roll continued with forward pressure to hold the nose up as the aircraft approaches the inverted attitude. The roll is again stopped inverted and then aileron is suddenly reapplied until the wings-vertical position. The forward pressure has been replaced with a large amount of top rudder. The last part sees the roll supported by back pressure as the rudder is centered.

Points of Airmanship

The hesitation roll is relatively straightforward. Concentration is high and look out is almost impossible to maintain. The aileron inputs are easy but it takes a little practice to coordinate the rudder and elevator inputs.

Snap Roll

Description

In the snap roll, the aircraft is caused to depart from controlled flight by stalling one wing during an accelerated pull up. Full rudder, and usually full aileron, assist the rotation.

It is effectively a one-turn horizontal spin.

Opposite aileron, or sometimes normal spin recovery controls, are applied to stop the roll after a half or one turn. It is an easy and quite comfortable maneuver provided the entry speed is kept low. The aircraft can be damaged by snap rolls at too high a speed as not only are the g forces higher, the side loads on the vertical stabilizer and rudder are also very high. The best place for a snap roll is from inverted to inverted at the top of a loop when the airspeed is low and decreasing, the flight path is initially upward, there is altitude to spare, and all the forces are low. It works very well. It is also a fun variation of a Immelmann. There is also an outside snap roll induced from negative g or inverted flight, rather than a positive g, entry.

Piloting Technique

The snap roll from level flight is entered from low airspeed (the manufacturer will specify, or at least should recommend, a strict maximum speed for entering a snap roll—note that it is well below V_A). From level flight, some 10 knots or more below the limiting speed, raise the nose to the climb attitude, apply full power and then smoothly and simultaneously apply full rudder, full back stick and, after rotation starts, full aileron in the direction of the roll. You will feel the buffet and the stall of the down-going wing almost immediately. Hold the controls firmly to sustain the roll. To recover, center the ailerons, apply opposite rudder and release the back pressure to unstall the wings. The aircraft will stop rotating very quickly (much quicker than a spin recovery) due to the slipstream from the propeller over the rudder and elevators. If you are using a half snap roll to enter a split S or as the top of an Immelmann then you must allow for the fact that the snap roll through only 180° will leave you off-axis.

Points of Airmanship

Don't ever exceed the limiting speed and don't enter the maneuver if the aircraft is accelerating or descending. Only do it with a clear horizon and don't do it by half measures. The snap roll is a sudden, coarse, buffet, stall, roll, spin, recover, *"What happened?"* sort of maneuver. At the top of a loop, it is almost gentle in comparison. This maneuver is known as the *avalanche*.

Avalanche

Description

The avalanche is easy, safe and quite spectacular from the cockpit—as well as from the ground. It consists of a complete snap roll from the inverted attitude to the inverted attitude at the top of a normal loop.

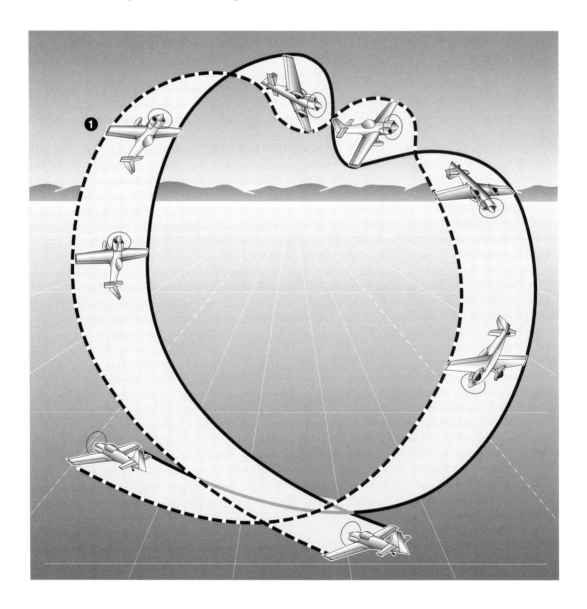

Piloting Technique

1. Simply enter a loop and, when the far horizon comes into sight toward the top of the loop, increase the back pressure until the buffet is noticeable and then apply full rudder.

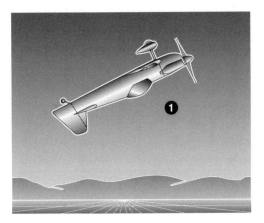
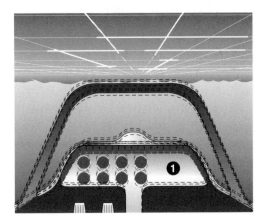

As the aircraft stalls, move the stick fully back. Centralize the stick and stop the roll with opposite rudder as it completes the roll toward the inverted position. The nose will now be below the horizon and it is then very easy to complete the loop.

It takes a conscious effort to pull through the buffet into the stall at the top of the loop. There is a tendency to leave it all too late and to end up steeply nose down. Start applying excessive back pressure as soon as the far horizon comes into the forward field-of-view.

Points of Airmanship

It is easy to become confused about the aircraft's attitude and direction during the snap roll as the horizon may not be in view. If there is any doubt, centralize the controls and recover from the dive. You may be steeply inverted at the completion of the roll. A pull through will consume a great amount of altitude and may result in excessive speed. Roll to the nearest horizon and recover. Adjust the throttle and RPM as required.

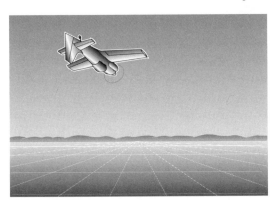
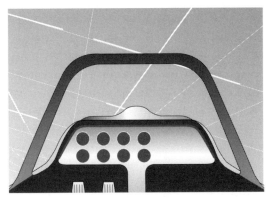

Derry Turn

Description

The Derry turn was named after the test pilot, John Derry, who used the maneuver to demonstrate a heavy jet fighter at Farnborough (England).

The maneuver consists of a steep turn in one direction reversed via a roll under— through the inverted position to a steep turn in the opposite direction.

The roll itself is nominally an aileron roll but depending on airspeed, large amounts of rudder may be required to counter the adverse yaw and the maneuver can be most unbalanced. It sounds simple and it looks spectacular in a heavy fighter, especially at lower speeds, but it can be fraught with danger near the ground.

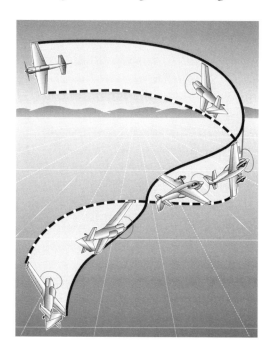

Piloting Technique

Start from a normal steep turn with full power. A visual feature may be used for the reversal. When there is about 15° to go, relax the back pressure and roll the aircraft under with full aileron and proverse rudder until the opposite 60° bank angle is reached. Stop the roll and reapply the *g*. Simple.

Points of Airmanship

It is essential to release the back pressure before applying the aileron and rudder or you suddenly have full pro-spin controls. Further, imagine if the airspeed is low. . .

Precision Spin

Description

Some pilots like to include a controlled one-and-a-half turn spin as part of their aerobatic repertoire. The essential aspect of this maneuver is to start and complete the rotations precisely on heading. This requires a positive entry and recovery. This, in turn, means practice and being familiar with your particular airplane.

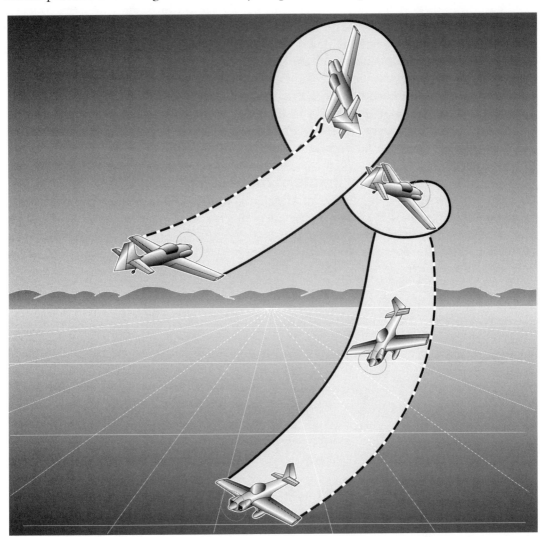

Most aircraft have not yet stabilized in 1½ turns, so there is less momentum (gyroscopic moments) and there is a more positive, and more immediate, recovery. The entry is the same as the snap roll but without aileron input and without power (the throttle is closed on entry) followed by a delayed, but anticipated, recovery.

Piloting Technique

Start from straight-and-level at 10 knots above V_S. The top of a wing-over or chandelle gives a good position and energy level and allows a good lookout. Enter the spin with full-back stick, throttle closed and full rudder—and hold the control inputs firmly. The aircraft will stall and auto-rotate.

Keep track of your heading and apply full spin recovery controls—center the stick and apply full opposite rudder. The aircraft will quickly stop rotating and will accelerate downwards. Recover normally from the dive, tracking your line feature on the ground.

Most aircraft will stop rotating within one quarter to one half turn, and this will determine when spin recovery controls are applied. Recovery needs to be positive and then the aircraft is recovered on line from the ensuing dive.

Points of Airmanship

It is important to have distinct ground references for direction during the entry and recovery. It is equally important to have a clearly defined horizon. If the aircraft does not recover immediately, maintain the recovery controls and wait. If you become disoriented, hold the controls and wait for the airspeed to increase. Then look for the horizon and recover from the dive.

Chapter 7

An Aerobatic Sequence

Developing an aerobatic sequence is not only challenging but makes better use of airborne time, better use of airspace and gives a better opportunity to develop anticipation and orientation. Also, the best way to return to aerobatic flying after a break is to have your own flight sequence of maneuvers, which you can perform and develop until it becomes polished and professional. You can develop a second, more advanced sequence for later stages when you are more current. Further, your own sequence will reflect your own taste, skill and preferences.

Designing the Sequence

Start with a piece of paper and draw a line representing the axis of the sequence which will be the reference line feature on the ground. Choose a feature into the wind or, otherwise, accept any displacement that occurs during the duration of the sequence. You may use your own symbols or perhaps you would like to adopt the now universal code for aerobatics, called the Aresti system of notation. Choose, say, five core maneuvers that will be linked. Let's take an example:

- Take a loop, barrel roll, aileron roll, hammerhead, slow roll with a pause at the inverted position, and an avalanche. Use the hammerhead as a linking maneuver and even add another one, if desired.
- From the line feature, plan to start with potential energy of say 2,000 feet above the minimum altitude and run in at 90° to the reference line so that you can have a good look for other aircraft.
  The HASELL checks will be done well before this.

In this example, all maneuvers are easier to the left and with side-by-side seating so you will plan to begin with a wing-over to the left to line up with the feature and at the same time set the attitude and power and establish the entry speed for the first maneuver. You can better see other traffic, too.

The easiest maneuver to begin with, and the one with the lowest entry speed, is the aileron roll. From a left wing-over it doesn't matter which way you roll as there will be a pause for a straight pull up before the roll.

- From the left roll, pause and then pull–up into a right-hand wing-over through 225° to offset the line for a pull up into a left-hand barrel roll.
- From the barrel roll, continue directly into a left wing-over to line up on the feature for a loop.

- The exit dive from a loop is a good entry point for a hammerhead—which is easier to the left.
- From the hammerhead pull up smoothly into an avalanche and a further hammerhead.
- Exit from the hammerhead will be controlled to contain the airspeed and pull up slightly, pause and then roll to inverted, pause for 5 seconds and roll erect. To provide a deliberate ending to the sequence, waggle the wings to indicate you are complete when the aircraft is straight–and–level and all applied g is removed.

What Do You Think?

A sequence can be hard work but good fun and great training. The whole sequence would have taken about 5 minutes. Once the sequence is designed, consider if the continuity and flow is OK—and if the direction of the maneuvers allows for a smooth flow. Modify if necessary and then pace it out on the ground.

Draw Mud-Maps and Do a Rain Dance

Practice the sequence on the ground by walking through the sequence around a line in the dirt—a true *mud-map* of your aerobatic sequence—and saying the maneuvers attitudes, entry speeds and power settings as you go. It's a wonderful way to ingrain the sequence and the necessary actions. Include where to look in your rehearsal and say the sequence out loud. This is called *over-learning* and *part-task training*. It is a known and valuable learning process.

Aresti Notation

Colonel Jose Aresti was a world-renowned competition aerobatic pilot who approached flying in a scientific manner. He developed a notation for maneuvers which has become the international standard. It has been expanded to include a scoring system with degree of difficulty applied to each maneuver.

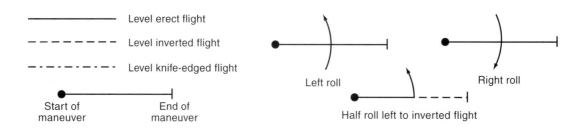

The Aresti notation includes a particular type of line to represent the aircraft's attitude and then a series of symbols to illustrate the particular maneuver as follows.

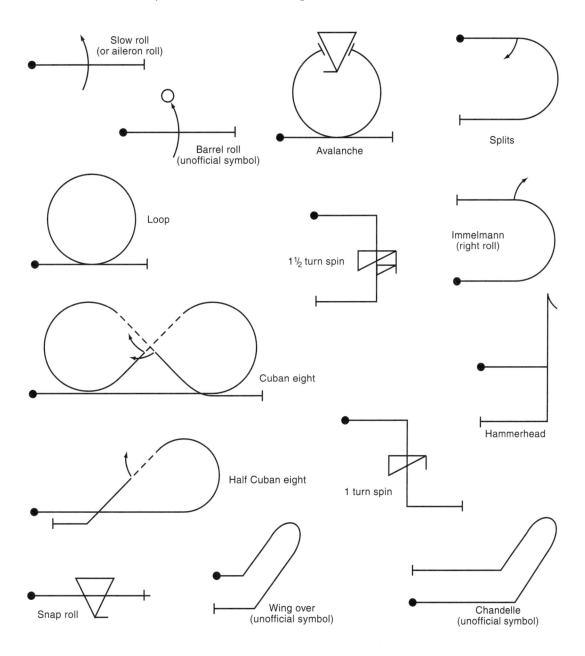

Slow roll
(or aileron roll)

Barrel roll
(unofficial symbol)

Avalanche

Splits

Loop

1½ turn spin

Immelmann
(right roll)

Cuban eight

Half Cuban eight

1 turn spin

Hammerhead

Snap roll

Wing over
(unofficial symbol)

Chandelle
(unofficial symbol)

If we wanted to illustrate the sequence we used above, it would look like this:

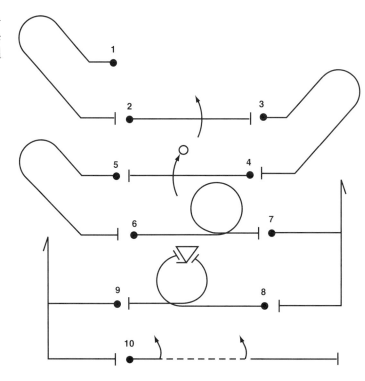

Performing the Sequence

Tips

- Use a ground reference line—into wind.
- A clear horizon all round.
- Use wing-overs early.
- Use the wing-overs to position, look out, and establish the line, the attitude and the entry speed for the next maneuver.
- Don't fuss too much with altitude as long as you are comfortably above 1,500 feet. (don't pull hard to be out by say 2,000 feet if the induced drag will prejudice the entry speed for the next maneuver).
- Use left wing-over into right roll so it flows—and right roll into right wing-over.
- Plan the wing-over to position for the entry to a barrel roll, for example, loop into right wing-over into left barrel roll (225° change of direction).
- If things fall apart, return to straight-and-level. Don't fly from one error and allow it to compound into the next.
- Start with excess altitude rather than finish with inadequate energy.
- If you can't make the entry speed by the required altitude, stop and climb and start again. Never start a maneuver with inadequate energy and expect to stagger through it.

Chapter 8

A Basic Aerobatic Training Program

Introduction

The following program was developed over a number of years and is popular, as it offers a gentle and controlled introduction to aerobatics and allowed the student to develop a tolerance, understanding, feel and expectation for maneuvering, at the same time as the skills and knowledge of the aircraft are developed. It was developed around the CAP 10 airplane but it may be that for your aircraft type, a different sequence of increasingly difficult maneuvers may be appropriate.

There may also be a need to conduct an initial tailwheel conversion.

Teaching Aerobatics

The student will become confident if you are and it shows. Don't try to teach unless you are current in the aircraft type and the maneuvers.

If you love flying and you love aerobatics, the student will also—it's as simple as that. If you criticize some aircraft types or avoid some maneuvers, the student will inherit the same bias and caution.

Don't try to impress the student with your ability. Try to teach him or her so well that the student impresses you with their ability to fly—and therefore reflects your ability to instruct.

Don't scare them and don't let them scare themselves (or you) until they have a degree of proficiency and you are sure they will ultimately cope with the developing situation.

Coax them through the exercises and encourage them. Don't be over-critical until they are consistently safe and you know their ability should produce more accurate or polished results.

Always promote early recognition and correction of potential loss-of-control and completion of the maneuver rather than a series of unusual attitude recoveries—although they must be fully capable of ultimately recovering from such situations.

Pick a progression of demand and difficulty that they can show improvement and competence. It is easy to set a task that is beyond them and so reduce their confidence and pleasure. There will be the occasional over-confident student but they will soon realize the reality as you let them progress to more difficult exercises. Fairly criticize any acceptance of standards that are less than those of which they are capable. If their confidence exceeds their ability, the aircraft and the maneuvers will show it.

One way is to progress from a steep turn to a wing-over, to an aileron roll from a wing-over entry, then to a loop, barrel roll and inverted flight. Then join some basic maneuvers together in a short sequence. Use a line feature into wind.

Overview of the Aerobatic Training Program

To develop confidence, piloting skill and a tolerance to maneuvering, your school should approach the training program in a logical and safe way. They will first refresh your flying at low speed and high angles-of-attack, high speed and low angles-of-attack, and, for the first time, high speed and high angles-of-attack.

They'll begin with a refresher on steep turns and managing the energy of the aircraft in sustained turning. You'll see what limits there are for your aircraft and explore flying at speeds above and below V_A. They'll progressively build up load factors and maneuver rates as you go along. A logical sequence to follow begins with a refresher on steep turns, and flying at low speed, high angle-of-attack, in both straight and level flight and turning.

They will also look at the highest speed end of the aircraft's flight envelope and, for the first time, high speed and high angle-of-attack. They'll conduct a refresher on unusual or extreme attitude recoveries, nose high and nose low, and look at stalling and departure from control flight. The value of doing these exercises is to refresh the feel and characteristics of the particular aircraft at the extremes of this flight envelope.

Then, they'll start the aerobatic course as such. The first and, probably, the most important maneuver, is the wing-over. The wing-over is the positioning and linking maneuver and is essential for all aerobatic sequences. It's also extremely valuable to introduce the behavior of the aircraft, as it accelerates, decelerates, nose high altitude, nose low altitude, high air speed, low air speed, and it's a wonderful refresher or a way of getting to know an aircraft type that you haven't flown before. From the wing-over, you'll progress to the simple aileron roll.

Next, the loop, the barrel roll and the hammerhead. Then you'll link these maneuvers together in a sequence, so that you can flow from one to the next.

When the positive g maneuvers are mastered, you'll gently explore inverted flight and the first of the negative g maneuvers, the slow roll.

Also look at joined maneuvers, and if the aircraft has sufficient performance, upward rolls and downward rolls. Then link rolling and looping maneuvers into the Cuban eight and the Immelmann.

Finally, you'll put these additional maneuvers, into one sequence. At this level, all of the maneuvers will be done in the training area, above 1,500 feet, and you will use a ground reference purely for orientation. No attempt will be made to position the sequence in relation to a point on the ground. For now, ignore the effect of wind.

Detailed Sequence of Instruction

A suggested program is detailed as follows:

Flight Zero—Tailwheel Endorsement (if appropriate)

Description
The introduction to a tailwheel configuration is an important first step for many aerobatic pilots. While the handling of the aircraft is identical, the takeoff, landing and the ground handling are significantly different. The tailwheel aircraft requires a greater degree of control and anticipation. This in itself is a valuable first step in becoming a competent aerobatic pilot.

Points of Airmanship
Prevent any yaw early. Fly accurate speeds, especially at the runway threshold. Discuss the appropriate technique for the aircraft (three-point or tail-down wheeler) and cross-wind techniques. Include sideslipping approaches if appropriate.

Flight One—Aircraft Type Familiarization or Refresher
The introduction to your aerobatic aircraft is a vital part of the aerobatic endorsement, and if this is shallow then you will become neither confident nor competent in the more demanding maneuvers. Take your time in getting to know the aircraft type thoroughly.

The introduction should include:
- familiarization with speeds, power settings and limitations;
- the flight envelope (V-n diagram);
- V_A;
- weight and balance;
- emergency procedures; and
- restarting the engine in flight.

The flight should include:
- familiarization with the aerobatic training area and routes;
- practice forced landings;
- maintaining balanced flight with airspeed and power changes and with aileron application at high and low airspeeds;
- high and low speed handling;
- maneuvering on the buffet/maneuvering at a set value of g;
- maneuvering at high angles-of-attack at high and low airspeeds;
- unusual attitude recoveries; and
- stalling and departures.

Description

Introduction to the wing-over and chandelle:

- power settings and trim;
- attitudes;
- using a line reference;
- progressively steeper wing-overs with more rapid control inputs and more extreme attitudes;
- completing the wing-over on line and with the entry attitude for a following maneuver; and
- alternate joined wing-overs.

Points of Airmanship

Hand-over/take-over procedures. Look out. Looking ahead of the maneuvers. Strapping-in. Sick bag. No loose objects. HASELL checks.

Flight Two—The Aileron Roll and Loop

Description

Having gained a degree of familiarity and confidence in maneuvering the aircraft and having developed a feel for the stall boundary, the next step is to turn the aircraft upside-down while maintaining positive g.

Depending on the aircraft type it may be easier to begin with the loop but if possible, the aileron roll is a softer introduction for the student. Use the wing-over as the clearing and set-up maneuver and build on the previous sortie.

Stress the importance of setting the trim and feeling the feedback through the controls. The loop needs a firm but not violent application of g, a straight pull up and then minor adjustment for balance, alignment and buffet. Look back early for the far horizon over the top and be ready to slightly relax the back pressure to avoid excessive buffet. Control the RPM and reinstate the back pressure as the aircraft accelerates.

The aileron roll can be entered as for the wing-over, and when the nose-high attitude is reached, stop the pitching and apply the aileron positively. In most trainers, full aileron will be needed. Simply complete the 360° rotation. Initially keep whatever fore or aft pressure was needed to check the pitching. Later, apply a little forward pressure from the 45° before, to 45° after the inverted attitude.

Points of Airmanship

The control inputs should now be firm and confident but not violent. Keep the head and eyes looking where the aircraft is going to be going. Stress the need for vertical space and a clear horizon. The look out needs to cover a larger area of sky, also vertically. Especially point out blind spots for the aircraft type. Review the physiological aspects of g.

Flight Three—The Barrel Roll and Hammerhead

Description

In may ways, this sortie is the most pleasant and yet the most challenging. Refresh the previous lesson and revisit the maneuvers.

The hammerhead is straightforward, having the same entry and the same recovery as the loop. Try for a truly vertical climb, or a little more, apply full rudder and then use aileron to prevent a roll into the direction of yaw. Control the RPM in the dive.

The likelihood with the barrel roll is that the entry attitude will not be high enough and the aircraft will lose a great deal of altitude through the second half of the roll. Also, there is a tendency to relax the aileron application, when it should be slightly increased with reducing airspeed. As a result, the roll rate will slow over the top. Increased back pressure combined with relaxed aileron is required for the last quarter of the roll. Balance is a finesse that will come with practice.

Points of Airmanship

Vertical recovery technique should be revised. Engine handling should be emphasized for the aircraft type. Actions in the event of the engine stopping should be discussed.

Flight Four—Half Rolls, Inverted Flight and the Complete Slow Roll

Description

Use the previously practiced entry to the aileron roll and stop the aircraft at the wings-level inverted position. Illustrate and maintain the inverted level flight attitude with forward stick. Stress the stick position and force required. Complete and aileron roll to erect flight, progressively relaxing the forward pressure to the wings vertical position and then applying slight back pressure for the last 90° of the roll.

The complete slow roll is best built with a pause at the inverted position to ensure that the second half starts from the correct point. The second half of the roll is the most difficult and if the correct inverted flight attitude is not achieved, it becomes impossible.

Points of Airmanship

This is the first flight with negative g, and it should be approached cautiously to maintain the student's confidence. A clean and tidy cockpit helps considerably. Emphasize strapping-in correctly and firmly. No loose objects.

Flight Five—The Cuban Eight, Immelmann and Avalanche

Description

The Cuban eight is a pleasant combination of the loop and aileron roll. The Immelmann requires a higher *g*, positive pull up and a higher entry speed. The roll should be commenced as the aircraft reaches the inverted flight attitude when full aileron and balancing rudder is applied. Adverse aileron yaw can be pronounced. The back pressure is removed immediately before the aileron is applied but don't try to apply the firm forward pressure required for inverted flight.

The Avalanche is an exciting and easy maneuver to perform. Emphasize the benefit of accelerating the aircraft into the buffet and stall well before the inverted flight attitude.

Points of Airmanship

Two areas which offer a risk of departure are the Immelmann when full aileron and significant rudder is applied at very low airspeed. It is important that the back pressure is removed so that the angle-of-attack is not close to the stalling angle when the roll is commenced. The snap roll at the top of the avalanche is safe if it is commenced early and the aircraft is pulled positively into the buffet. It should not be commenced when the inverted attitude is past as the airspeed will build quickly and the aircraft limits may be exceeded. There is a risk of disorientation during the roll and it is initially difficult to recover to the line feature.

Flight Six—A Basic Aerobatic Sequence

Description

The greatest pleasure in flying comes from a practiced and controlled aerobatic sequence, not unlike a choreographed aerial ballet. Use a line feature and stress the need for anticipation. Always be thinking ahead to the next maneuver.

Points of Airmanship

Emphasize firm but gentle control. Look out. Think ahead of the aircraft—feel the cues. Use a line feature and a clear horizon. Discuss escape routes from any and every stage of the sequence.

Afterword

Advanced Maneuvering

The intention of this book is to interest and possibly excite you enough to enter the world of aerobatic flight. If you are already inspired, I need say no more. You may be happy to stay at the stage of flying aerobatics for pleasure, or you may wish to proceed further to competition and advanced maneuvers. If you do, I recommend Neil Williams' excellent book, *Aerobatics*, published by Airlife. Also contact the International Aerobatic Club and Mudry Aviation on the Internet.

Now that you have become competent at basic aerobatic maneuvers, I would also like to add a word of caution—the next step is a *doosie*. You must not, cannot, should not, please don't, attempt advanced or ground referenced maneuvers without experience and without specialized instruction. These maneuvers are beyond the skill-level of most pilots—including airline pilots and military pilots without special training. This is the realm of the specialist competition and display pilot, and it's a profession of its own.

Maneuvering Relative to the Ground—The Effects of Wind

When aerobatics are performed for a judge or for a crowd, then they have to be oriented to a reference line on the ground and one that is unlikely to be into wind. Thus, all maneuvers have to be modified by continuously changing conditions. A loop becomes an offset loop—one wing up, one wing down. The aircraft has to track down a reference line which is not aligned with the roll-axis of the aircraft. You are not allowed to fly over the crowd, yet, sure-as-eggs, the wind will blow you towards the crowd during your low level turns, so that you are flying to the limit to stay clear—and the induced drag is spoiling your excess energy. Add to this excitement, stress, nerves—and stir gently. You can see that this is a special arena that needs special skills.

Competitive Aerobatics

You will enjoy basic aerobatic maneuvers and some of you will become addicts. The next steps to competition aerobatics are progressive. The International Aerobatic Club (IAC) and the Experimental Aircraft Association (EAA) have advisory groups on how to progress on to low or high level aerobatic competition. There are categories for basic, intermediate and advanced pilots at national and, ultimately, international levels. For these you need a seriously capable aerobatic ship.

Many pilots who pursue aerobatics as a sport also participate in competitive events. These events provide an opportunity for pilots to match their skills against an established criteria or standard of grading. Aerobatic competitions are held throughout the world and are sponsored by various aviation organizations. The events are conducted according to the rules and regulations established by the various organizations and are usually monitored by the FAA. The Aerobatic Competency Evaluation (ACE) program was created by the air show industry with oversight by FAA and Transport Canada. It outlines the standards by which the competency/safety of air show pilots are evaluated, and recommendations are made to the FAA and Transport Canada for the issuance of the appropriate aerobatic competency/safety credentials.

You can find out more about the different classes of aerobatic competitions both at the national and international levels by contacting ones of the following organizations:
- Experimental Aircraft Association (EAA), http://www.eaa.org
- International Aerobatic Club (IAC), http://acro.harvard.edu/IAC/iac_homepg.html
- International Council of Air Shows, http://www.airshows.org

Back to Earth

Enough of these future possibilities—let's go back to our basic aerobatic maneuvers at a safe altitude. Everyone that has ever been a good and complete pilot started here. Learn them well. Take care of yourself and your aircraft.

I know you'll enjoy it as much as I.

"What is chiefly needed is skill rather than machinery."
Wilbur Wright (1900)